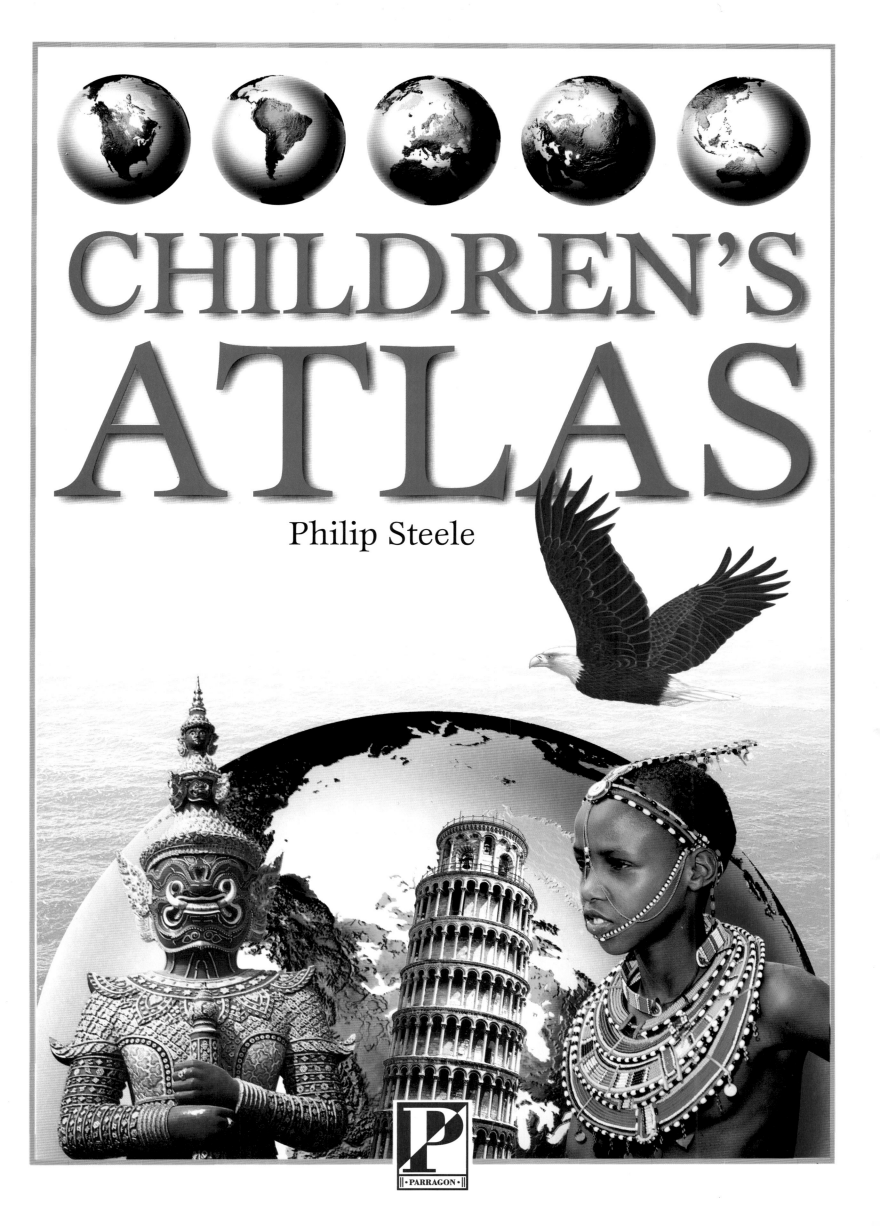

CHILDREN'S ATLAS

Philip Steele

PARRAGON

This edition published by Parragon, 1999
Parragon,
Queen Street House, 4 Queen Street, Bath, BA1 1HE

2 4 6 8 10 9 7 5 3

Produced by
Miles Kelly Publishing Ltd,
Bardfield Centre, Great Bardfield, Essex, CM7 4SL

© Copyright Dempsey Parr 1998

Printed in Spain

ISBN 0 75253 091 7

Design: Full Steam Ahead
Cartographic editor: Keith Lye
Cartography: Digital Wisdom
Artwork commissioning: Branka Surla
Project manager: Kate Miles
Additional help from Susanne Grant and Lynne French
Reprographics: DPI Colour Ltd

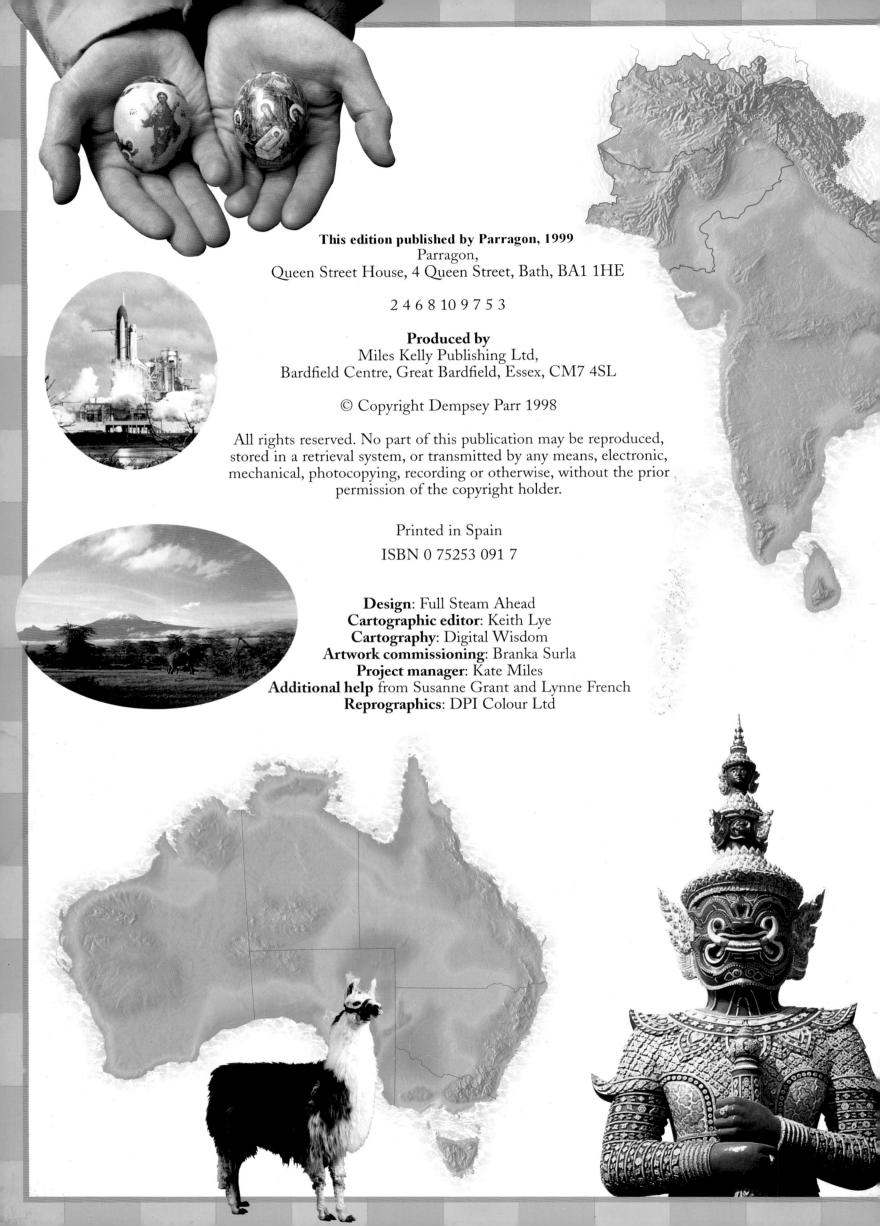

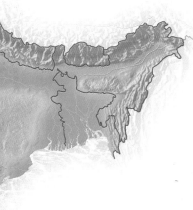

CONTENTS

HOW TO USE THIS ATLAS

WELCOME TO THE PLANET EARTH! This atlas shows you the world we live in. An atlas is any large book of maps. Maps are plans which show the surface of a planet as if it was flat, instead of round. They show the lie of the land, the rivers and coastlines, mountains and seas.

Maps which just show the details of the landscape are called 'physical'. Maps which just show the borders of countries, states, counties or provinces are called 'political'. The maps in this book show the physical details of the land, but they show national borders and major cities as well. Maps use signs and symbols to give you more information. Look at the key to find out what they mean.

So how do you find the city or country you are looking for? First of all look up the name you want in the index on p.61. When you have found the right page, look for the name on the big map of the region. Next to each regional map, look for the little map which helps you to see at a glance which part of the world is being shown.

Next, read the words to find out more about the countries, the climate of the region, the peoples and how they live. Small boxes also give you key facts and figures about each of the countries. They tell you the area, the population size, the name of the capital city, the country's official language or languages and the currency, or type of money, used by the people there.

When you read about distant lands, it may help to compare them with where you live. Are they bigger or smaller, hotter or wetter, more crowded? You might use the maps to do a bit of detective work. Can you work out why most Australian cities are near the coast, or why most Canadian cities are in the south of the country?

Colours
On this map the different colours show you at a glance the physical features of the landscape. Each colour represents a type of geographic feature.

Spot the mountain
This symbol means 'mountain'. The mountain's name is printed next to it, along with the height of the summit above sea level. The height is given in metres.

N for north
This symbol represents a compass, with its magnetic needle pointing due north.

N

Capital cities
The most important town in any country is called the capital city. This is very often the biggest town and is normally where the government makes the laws. Some capitals, however, are quite small.

Coastlines and borders
The borders of Japan are natural, because the country is made up of islands. Other countries may have land borders, marked by a line on the map.

Where in the world
If you want to find out where the regional map fits into a map of the whole world, check these small circular maps. The areas coloured in red show the location.

Key to symbols

- ■ Capitals
- ● Towns
- — Rivers
- — Borders
- Lakes
- Mountains

Map labels: La Pérouse Strait, Rebun I., Rishiri I., Wakkanai, Teshio, Kuril Is. (Russia), Ishikari Bay, Ishikari, Asahigawa, Hokkaido, Asahi Mt. 2,290 m, Otaru, Sapporo, Obihiro, Kushiro, Muroran, Uchiura Bay, Erimo Cape, Hakodate, Tsugaru Strait, Mutsa Bay, Aomori, SEA OF JAPAN, Hirosaki, Hachinohe, Akita, Morioka, Kitakami, Kamaishi, Sakata, Yamagata, Sendai, Niigata, Sado, Fukushima, Nagaoka, Koriyama, Abukuma, Shinano, JAPAN, Iwaki, Hitachi, Toyama, Ueda, Utsunomiya, Mito, Kanazawa, Takasaki, JAPANESE ALPS, Fukui, Matsumoto, Tokyo, Oki Is., Takefu, Kofu, Kawasaki, Chiba, Gifu, Biwa Lake, Nagoya, Toyota, Mt. Fuji 3,776 m, Yokohama, Kyoto, Kobe, Shizuoka, Sagami Bay, Matsue, Honshu, Okayama, Osaka, Hamamatsu, O-shima, Hiroshima, Sakai, Matsusaka, Tsushima, Inland Sea, Takamatsu, Miyake I., Kitakyushu, Suo Sea, Tokushima, Wakayama, Kii Channel, PACIFIC OCEAN, Fukuoka, Matsuyama, Shikoku, Sasebo, Bungo Channel, Kochi, Hachijo I., Omuta, Kumamoto, Nagasaki, Amakusa Is., Kyushu, Sendai, Miyazaki, Koshiki Is., Kagoshima, Tanega, Yaku

INTRODUCTION

EARTH FACTS

The world we live in is a huge ball of rock and metal spinning around, or rotating, in space. As the planet Earth rotates, it travels around the Sun, held on its path by a pulling force called gravity. The Earth is one of nine planets circling the Sun, and together they make up the Solar System.

When we see pictures of Earth taken from space, our planet appears blue, white and brown. The blue is the colour of the seas and oceans which cover over two-thirds of the Earth's surface. The swirling white patterns are the clouds – water vapour which hangs in the air, or atmosphere, surrounding the Earth's surface. The brown is the colour of the ground, which is divided into the Earth's landmasses or continents.

Photographs of the Earth's surface taken from space zoom in to show even more details – the world's great river systems, the high mountain ranges, the sprawling cities and the patchwork of crops that feed the hungry mouths of the world's population, which is expected to reach over 6,100 million by the year 2000.

PLANET EARTH
Circumference around the Equator: 40,075 kilometres
Circumference around the Poles: 40,008 kilometres
Diameter at the Equator: 12,756 kilometres
Surface area: About 510,000,000 square kilometres
Area covered by sea: 71 percent
Average distance from the Sun: 149,600,000 kilometres
Average distance from the Moon: 385,000 kilometres
Period of rotation: 23 hours 56 minutes
Speed of rotation: 1,660 kilometres per hour at the Equator
Period of revolution: 365 days 6 hours
Speed of revolution: 29.8 kilometres per second

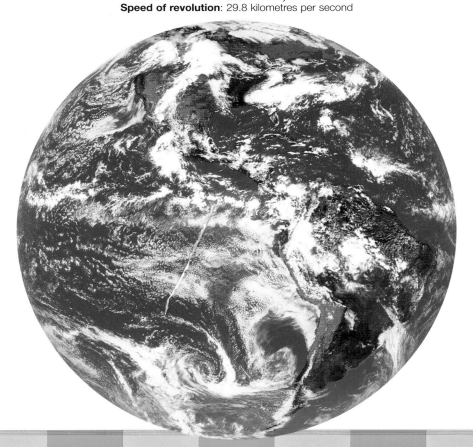

FACT BOX

The world's highest peak
Mount Everest or Qomolangma, between Nepal and China, is the highest point on the Earth's surface.

HIGHEST PEAKS

Mountain	Height	Location
Everest (Qomolangma)	8,848 m	China-Nepal
K2 (Qogir Feng)	8,611 m	India-Pakistan
Kanchenjunga	8,586 m	India-Nepal
Makalu 1	8,463 m	China-Nepal
Dhaulagiri 1	8,167 m	Nepal
Nanga Parbat	8,125 m	India
Annapurna 1	8,091 m	Nepal
Gosainthan (Xixabangma Feng)	8,012 m	China
Distaghil Sar	7,885 m	India
Nanda Devi	7,816 m	India

LONGEST RIVERS

River	Length	Location
Nile	6,670 km	North Africa
Amazon	6,448 km	South America
Chang Jiang (Yangtze)	6,300 km	Central China
Mississippi-Missouri-Red	6,020 km	North America
Yenisey-Angara-Selenga	5,540 km	Mongolia-Russia
Huang He	5,464 km	Northern China
Ob-Irtysh	5,409 km	Russia-Kazakhstan
Zaïre (Congo)	4,700 km	Central Africa
Lena-Kirenga	4,400 km	Russia
Mekong	4,350 km	Southeast Asia

LARGEST LAKES

Lake	Area	Location
Caspian Sea	371,800 sq km	Central Asia
Superior	82,103 sq km	USA-Canada
Victoria	69,484 sq km	East Africa
Aral Sea	65,500 sq km	Central Asia
Huron	59,569 sq km	USA-Canada
Michigan	57,757 sq km	USA-Canada
Tanganyika	32,893 sq km	East Africa
Baikal	31,449 sq km	Russia
Great Bear	31,328 sq km	Canada
Malawi	28,878 sq km	Southern Africa

LARGEST ISLANDS

Island	Area
Greenland	2,1830 sq km
New Guinea	821,000 sq km
Borneo	727,900 sq km
Madagascar	589,081 sq km
Baffin	509,214 sq km
Sumatra	431,982 sq km
Honshu	228,204 sq km
Great Britain	218,800 sq km
Victoria	212,200 sq km
Ellesmere	196,917 sq km

MAJOR WATERFALLS

Highest Waterfalls

	Height	Location
Angel Falls	979 m	Venezuela
Mardsalsfossen	774 m	Norway
Yosemite	739 m	United States

Waterfall	Greatest volume Volume	Location
Boyoma	17,000 cu m per sec	Dem. Rep. Congo (Zaïre)

OCEANS

Name	Area
Pacific	166,242,000 sq km
Atlantic	106,000,000 sq km
Indian	73,500,000 sq km
Arctic	14,350,000 sq km

COUNTRIES OF THE WORLD

To the glory of God
Places of worship vary greatly around the world. This Christian cathedral, St Basil's, was built in the 1500s in Moscow, capital of today's Russian Federation.

There are 192 countries in the world that are recognized as 'independent' nations, which means that they govern themselves. Many other lands are colonies or 'dependencies', which means that they are governed by other nations. The numbers change very often, as one country joins up with another one, or another splits up into separate nations. For example Eritrea was part of Ethiopia until 1991, when it broke away to become an independent nation.

Some countries are huge, some are tiny. The Russian Federation is the largest, with an area of 17,078,005 square kilometres. The smallest is Vatican City, at just 0.4 square kilometres. Some countries are home to just one people, while others are made up of many different peoples or ethnic groups, each with their own way of life and customs. Some peoples have no national borders of their own. For example the traditional homeland of the Kurdish people is divided between Turkey, Iraq and Iran.

The peoples of the world live very different lives. They have different faiths and beliefs, eat different foods and speak over 5000 different languages. Some people are very poor while others are very rich. However, the people on our planet also have many things in common. The spread of radio, television and other communications links in recent years has made the world a smaller place. Once it took years to travel around the world, but today we can get on a plane or keep in touch with each other at the push of a button.

Most of the world's countries are linked by agreements or treaties. Many European countries belong to the European Union, while African nations belong to the Organization of African Unity. Nearly all countries belong to the United Nations, which tries to prevent conflict and to build links between the world's nations.

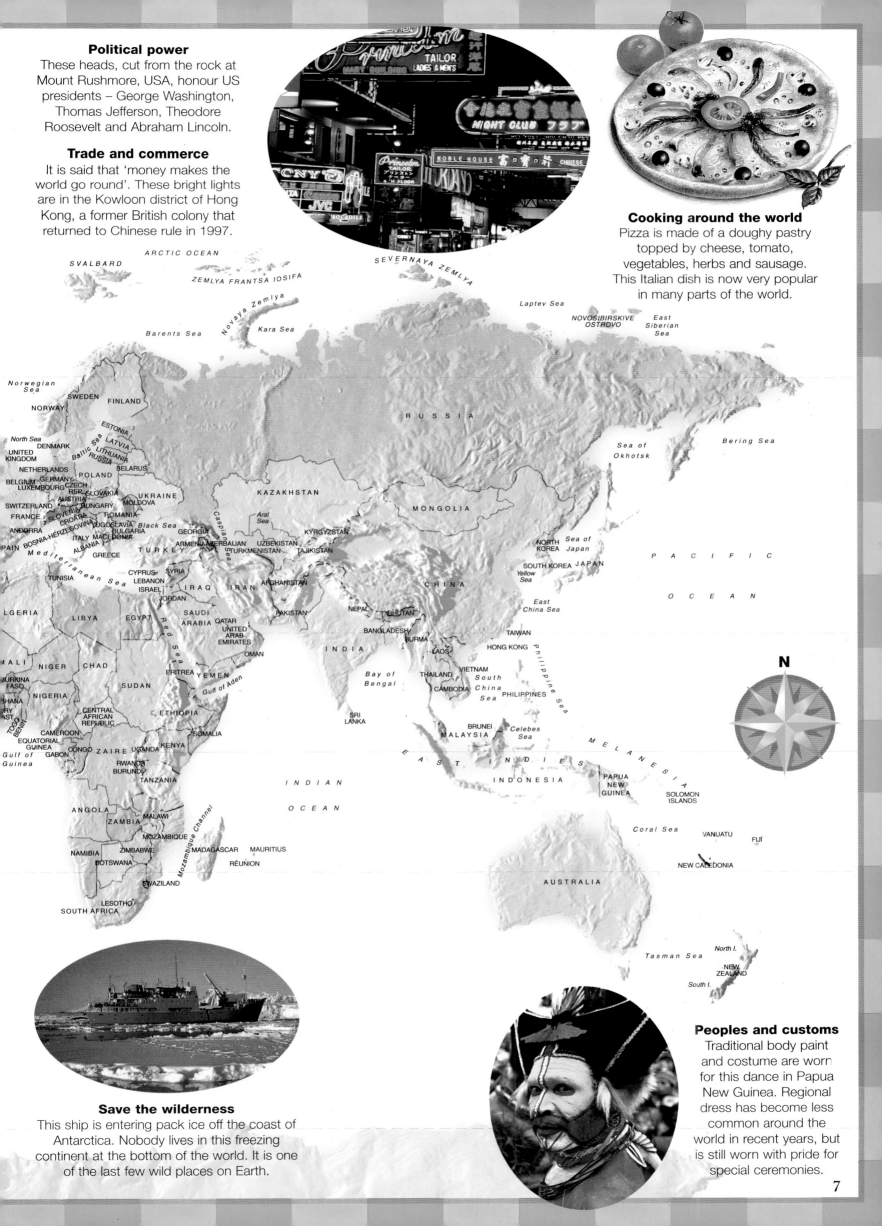

Political power
These heads, cut from the rock at Mount Rushmore, USA, honour US presidents – George Washington, Thomas Jefferson, Theodore Roosevelt and Abraham Lincoln.

Trade and commerce
It is said that 'money makes the world go round'. These bright lights are in the Kowloon district of Hong Kong, a former British colony that returned to Chinese rule in 1997.

Cooking around the world
Pizza is made of a doughy pastry topped by cheese, tomato, vegetables, herbs and sausage. This Italian dish is now very popular in many parts of the world.

Save the wilderness
This ship is entering pack ice off the coast of Antarctica. Nobody lives in this freezing continent at the bottom of the world. It is one of the last few wild places on Earth.

Peoples and customs
Traditional body paint and costume are worn for this dance in Papua New Guinea. Regional dress has become less common around the world in recent years, but is still worn with pride for special ceremonies.

N

7

SCANDINAVIA AND FINLAND

FACT BOX

◆ **Denmark**
Area: 43,075 sq km
Population: 5,300,000
Capital: Copenhagen
Official language: Danish
Currency: Danish krone

◆ **Sweden**
Area: 449,790 sq km
Population: 8,000,000
Capital: Stockholm
Official language: Swedish
Currency: Krona

◆ **Norway**
Area: 323,895 sq km
Population: 4,400,000
Capital: Oslo
Official language: Norwegian
Currency: Norwegian krone

◆ **Finland**
Area: 337,030 sq km
Population: 5,100,000
Capital: Helsinki
Official language: Finnish
Currency: Markka

TWO PENINSULAS extend from northwestern Europe, shaped rather like the claws of a crab. The southern peninsula, extending from Germany, is called Jutland.

Together with a chain of islands which includes Fyn, Sjælland, and Lolland, Jutland makes up the nation of **Denmark**. Most of Denmark is flat and low-lying, a country of green farmland. It exports bacon and dairy products.

Across the windy channels of Sgagerrak and Kattegat, between the North and Baltic Seas, lies the long northern peninsula occupied by **Sweden** and **Norway**. This is a land shaped by movements of ice in prehistoric times. Glaciers carved out the deep sea inlets called fjords along its ragged western coast. Ranges of mountains run down the peninsula like a backbone. They descend to a land of forests, bogs and thousands of lakes.

Summers can be warm, but winters are bitterly cold, with heavy snow. Norway lives by fishing and its North Sea rigs make it Western Europe's largest producer of oil and natural gas. Sweden is a major exporter of timber, paper, wooden furniture and motor vehicles.

The three nations of Denmark, Sweden and Norway form the region of Scandinavia. It was from here that the seafarers known as Vikings set out about 1,200 years ago. The Vikings raided and settled the coasts of Western Europe, traded in Russia and the Middle East, settled Iceland and Greenland and even reached North America. Today's Danes, Swedes and Norwegians are all closely related, as are the Germanic languages that they speak.

The Arctic lands of northern Scandinavia are home to the Saami (or Lapps), a people who traditionally lived by herding reindeer. Their neighbours are the Finns and the Russians.

Finland is a land of lakes, with coasts on the Gulfs of Bothnia and Finland. Its forests make it a leading producer of wood pulp and paper. Helsinki is the capital.

ICELAND extend from northwestern

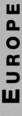

ICELAND

FINLAND

RUSSIA

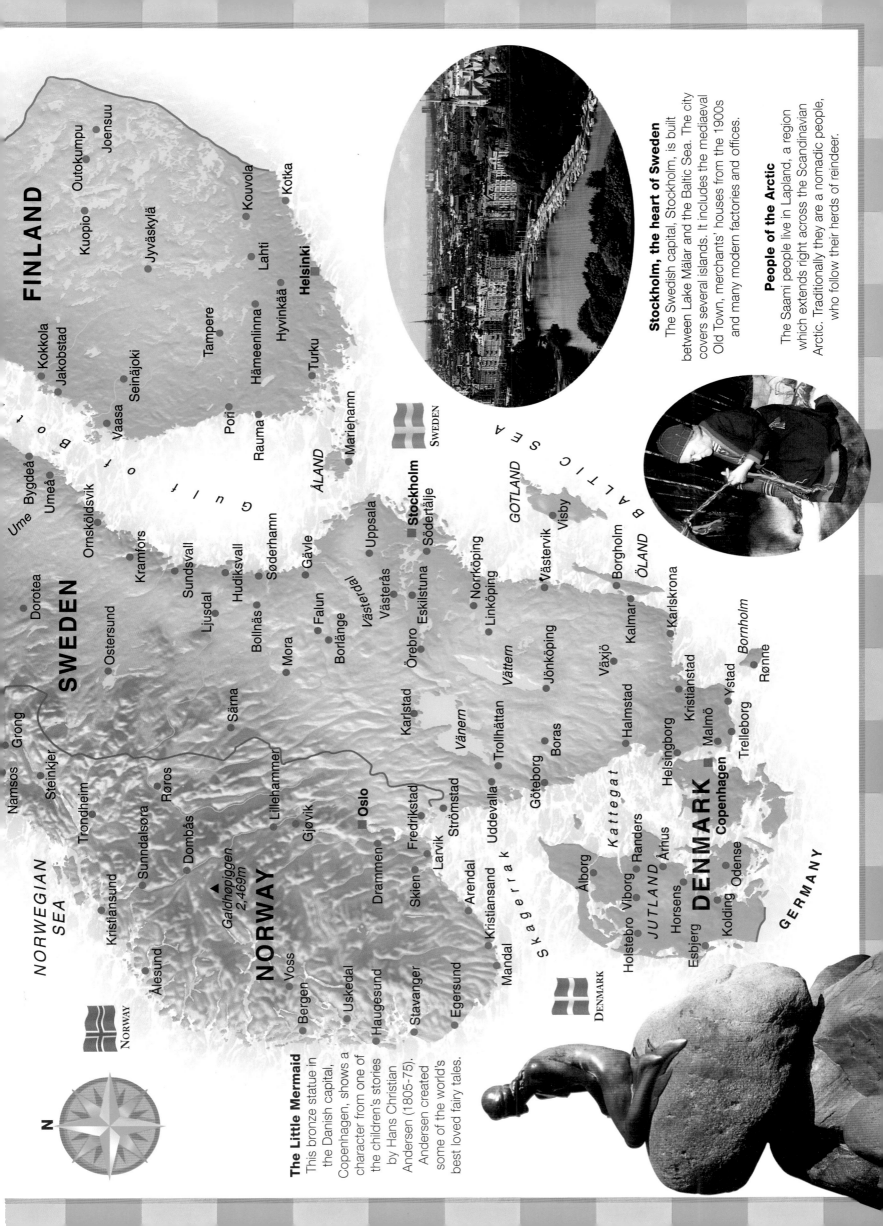

FINLAND

Outokumpu
Joensuu
Kuopio
Kouvola
Kotka
Jyväskylä
Lahti
Kokkola
Jakobstad
Tampere
Hyvinkää
Hämeenlinna
Helsinki
Seinäjoki
Vaasa
Turku
Pori
Rauma
Mariehamn
ÅLAND

Stockholm, the heart of Sweden

The Swedish capital, Stockholm, is built between Lake Mälar and the Baltic Sea. The city covers several islands. It includes the mediaeval Old Town, merchants' houses from the 1900s and many modern factories and offices.

People of the Arctic

The Saami people live in Lapland, a region which extends right across the Scandinavian Arctic. Traditionally they are a nomadic people, who follow their herds of reindeer.

SWEDEN

BALTIC SEA

SWEDEN

Ume Bygdeå
Umeå
Ornsköldsvik
Kramfors
Sundsvall
Hudiksvall
Söderhamn
Ljusdal
Bollnäs
Gävle
Falun
Mora
Borlänge
Östersund
Dorotea
Särna
GULF of BOTHNIA

Uppsala
Västerås
Stockholm
Södertälje
Eskilstuna
Örebro
Norrköping
Linköping
Västern
Vättern
Jönköping
Växjö
Visby
GOTLAND
Borgholm
ÖLAND
Västervik
Kalmar
Karlskrona
Kristianstad
Bornholm
Rønne

Namsos
Grong
Steinkjer
Trondheim
Sunndalsøra
Røros
Kristiansund
Ålesund
Voss
Bergen
Uskedal
Haugesund
Stavanger
Egersund

Dombås
Galdhøpiggen 2,469m
Lillehammer
Gjøvik
Oslo
Drammen
Fredrikstad
Skien
Larvik
Strömstad
Arendal
Kristiansand
Mandal

NORWAY

NORWEGIAN SEA

Särna
Karlstad
Trollhättan
Uddevalla
Göteborg
Boras
Halmstad
Helsingborg
Malmö
Ystad
Trelleborg
Skagerrak
Kattegat

Ålborg
Holstebro Viborg
Randers
Århus
Horsens
Esbjerg
Kolding Odense
JUTLAND
DENMARK
Copenhagen

DENMARK

GERMANY

The Little Mermaid

This bronze statue in the Danish capital, Copenhagen, shows a character from one of the children's stories by Hans Christian Andersen (1805-75). Andersen created some of the world's best loved fairy tales.

N

NORWAY

LOW COUNTRIES

THE COUNTRY OF THE NETHERLANDS is sometimes called Holland, but that is really the name of just two of its provinces, North and South Holland. This is a very flat, low-lying part of northern Europe. Long barriers and sea walls have been built to protect the countryside from North Sea floods. Large areas of land called polders have been reclaimed from the sea over the ages.

After a period under Spanish rule, the **Netherlands** became wealthy in the 1600s by trading with Southeast Asia. Its capital city, Amsterdam, still has many beautiful old houses and canals dating back to this golden age. The Netherlands today remain a centre of commerce, exporting bulbs and cut flowers, vegetables and dairy products, especially cheese, and also electrical goods. Rotterdam is the world's busiest seaport. Peoples of the Netherlands include the Dutch and the Frisians, as well as people whose families came from former Dutch colonies in Indonesia and Surinam.

The Flemish people of **Belgium** are closely related to the Dutch and their two languages are very similar. Belgium is also home to a French-speaking people, the Walloons, who mostly live in the south of the country. Much of the countryside in Belgium is also low and flat, but the land rises to the wooded hills of the Ardennes in the south. The country is heavily industrialized, and is also known for its fine foods – chocolates, pâtés, hams and traditional beers.

Luxembourg is a tiny country, a survivor of the age when most of Europe was divided into little states, principalities and duchies. However, modern industry and banking have made Luxembourg wealthy and successful. The people of Luxembourg speak French, German and a local language called Letzebuergesch.

The three countries have close ties. In 1948, after the terrible years of World War II (1939–45), Belgium, the Netherlands and Luxembourg set up an economic union called 'Benelux'. In 1957 they went on to what is now the European Union (EU).

Bruges skyline

The brick gables of old merchants' houses make a pleasing skyline in many historical towns of the Lowlands. Bruges has been famous through the ages for its lacemaking. The city is linked by canal to the seaport of Zeebrugge.

Wetlands butterfly

The Large Copper butterfly is on the endangered species list in both Belgium and the Netherlands. The butterfly thrives in flooded fields. Its caterpillar can survive underwater for many weeks. However draining of wetlands by farmers and roadbuilders threatens its survival.

NETHERLANDS

Emmen
Enschede
Almelo
Assen
Groningen
Meppel
Zwolle
Apeldoorn
Ijssel
Leeuwarden
Sneek
North-East Polder
Flevoland Polder
Amersfoort
Ameland
Terscheling
West Frisian Islands
Vlieland
Texel
Waddenzee
Barrier Dam
IJsselmeer
Markerwaard Polder (planned)
Hilversum
Amsterdam
Alkmaar
Zaanstad
Haarlem
Leiden

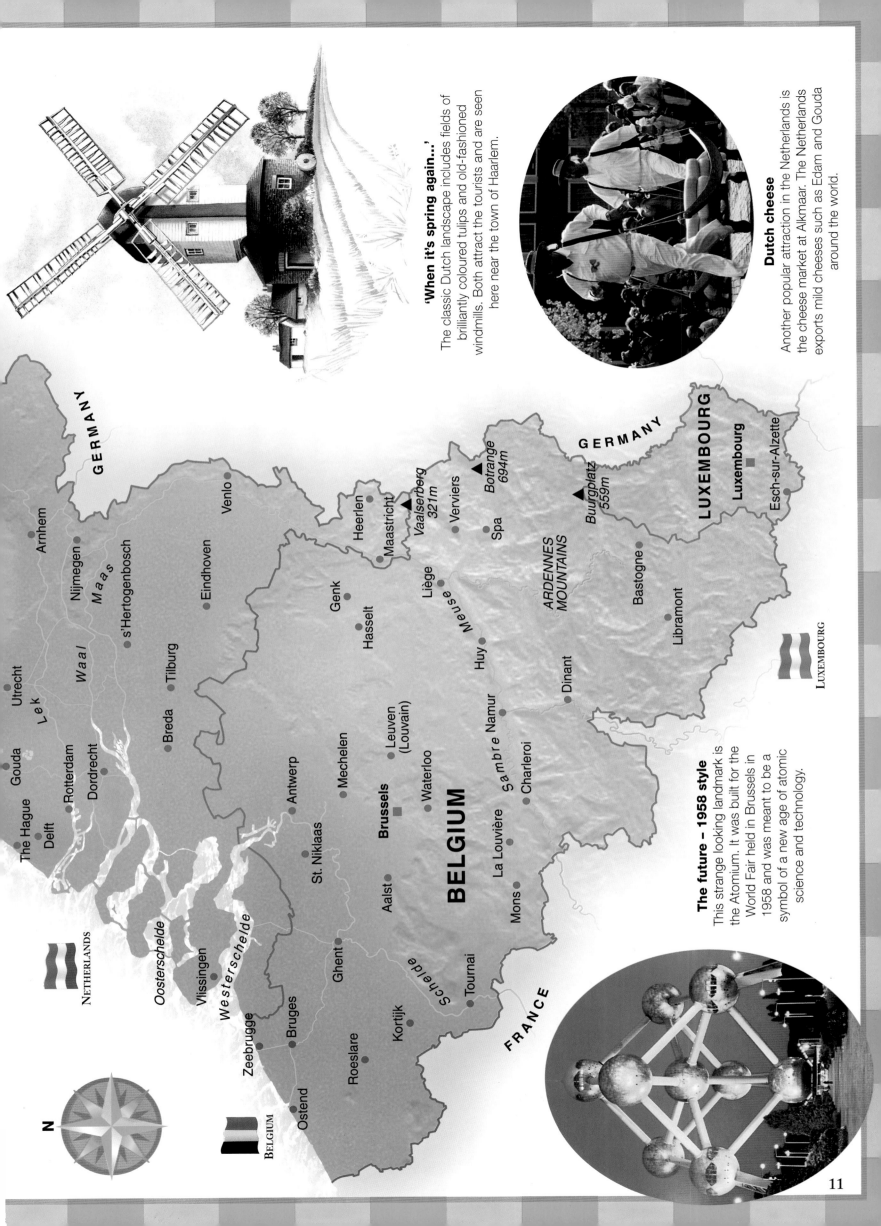

'When it's spring again...'
The classic Dutch landscape includes fields of brilliantly coloured tulips and old-fashioned windmills. Both attract the tourists and are seen here near the town of Haarlem.

Dutch cheese
Another popular attraction in the Netherlands is the cheese market at Alkmaar. The Netherlands exports mild cheeses such as Edam and Gouda around the world.

GERMANY

Arnhem

Nijmegen

Venlo

Heerlen

Maastricht

Vaalserberg
321m

Verviers

Botrange
694m

GERMANY

Spa

Buurgplatz
559m

LUXEMBOURG

Luxembourg

Esch-sur-Alzette

Liège

ARDENNES
MOUNTAINS

Bastogne

Libramont

Huy

Meuse

Dinant

LUXEMBOURG

Utrecht

Lek

Gouda

Rotterdam

Dordrecht

The Hague

Delft

Breda

Tilburg

s'Hertogenbosch

Eindhoven

Waal

Maas

Genk

Hasselt

Leuven
(Louvain)

Namur

Sambre

NETHERLANDS

Antwerp

Mechelen

Brussels

Waterloo

La Louvière

Charleroi

St. Niklaas

Aalst

Mons

BELGIUM

Ghent

Schelde

Tournai

Kortijk

Roeslare

Bruges

Zeebrugge

Ostend

BELGIUM

Oosterschelde

Westerschelde

Vlissingen

N

FRANCE

The future – 1958 style
This strange looking landmark is the Atomium. It was built for the World Fair held in Brussels in 1958 and was meant to be a symbol of a new age of atomic science and technology.

11

BRITISH ISLES

THE BRITISH ISLES lie off the northwestern coast of Europe, between the shallow waters of the North Sea and the stormy Atlantic Ocean. Their western shores are warmed by an ocean current called the North Atlantic Drift. The climate is mild, with a high rainfall in the west.

The largest island is called **Great Britain,** and its three countries (**England, Scotland** and **Wales**) are joined together within a United Kingdom. The second largest of the British Isles is called **Ireland.** Most of Ireland is an independent republic, but part of the north is governed as a province of the United Kingdom.

Great Britain has a landscape of rolling farmland. There are rugged highlands in Wales and Scotland, while England has rich farmland in the southeast, bleak moors in the north, flat fields in East Anglia and wild coasts in Cornwall. There are many beautiful old villages and towns, but also large cities and ports.

The Irish landscape is less crowded. It has green fields, misty hills and, in the west, steep cliffs pounded by Atlantic breakers. Its capital, Dublin, lies on the River Liffey.

English is spoken throughout the British Isles, but other languages may be heard too – Welsh, Irish and Scots Gaelic, and the various languages spoken by British people of Asian and African descent.

Both the UK and the **Republic of Ireland** are members of the European Union.

Wren

One of the most widespread birds of Britain, this short drab coloured bird with a cocked tail, has a loud warbling song. Wrens feed on caterpillars, beetles and bugs.

Highland games

Scottish pipers parade in the Highland Games. This competition has been taking place since the early nineteenth century, but has its roots in much older clan rivalries.

NORTH SEA

SHETLAND ISLANDS
Unst
Yell
Foula
Lerwick
Sumburgh Head
Fair Isle

Westray
Kirkwall
Hoy
South Ronaldsay
John o'Groats
ORKNEY ISLANDS

SCOTLAND

Fraserburgh
Peterhead
Aberdeen
Dee
Montrose
GRAMPIAN MTS.
Tay
Dundee
SIDLAW HILLS
Perth
Firth of Forth
OCHIL HILLS
Loch Lomond
Forth
Edinburgh
St. Abbs Head
Berwick-upon-Tweed
Holy I.
SCOTLAND
Glasgow
Tweed
Jedburgh
Clyde
CHEVIOT HILLS
Kilmarnock
SOUTHERN UPLANDS
Ayr
Arran

Cape Wrath
Thurso
Moray Firth
Inverness
Spey
Loch Ness
Don
NORTH WEST HIGHLANDS
Ben Nevis ▲ 1,343 m
Mallaig
Oban
Mull
Jura
Islay
Kintyre Pen.
NORTH

Butt of Lewis
North Minch
Stornoway
Lewis
Skye
Rhum
Coll
Tiree
INNER HEBRIDES
OUTER HEBRIDES
North Uist
South Uist
Barra

NORTHERN IRELAND
Malin Head
Rathlin I.
Giants
Tory I.
Aran I.

12

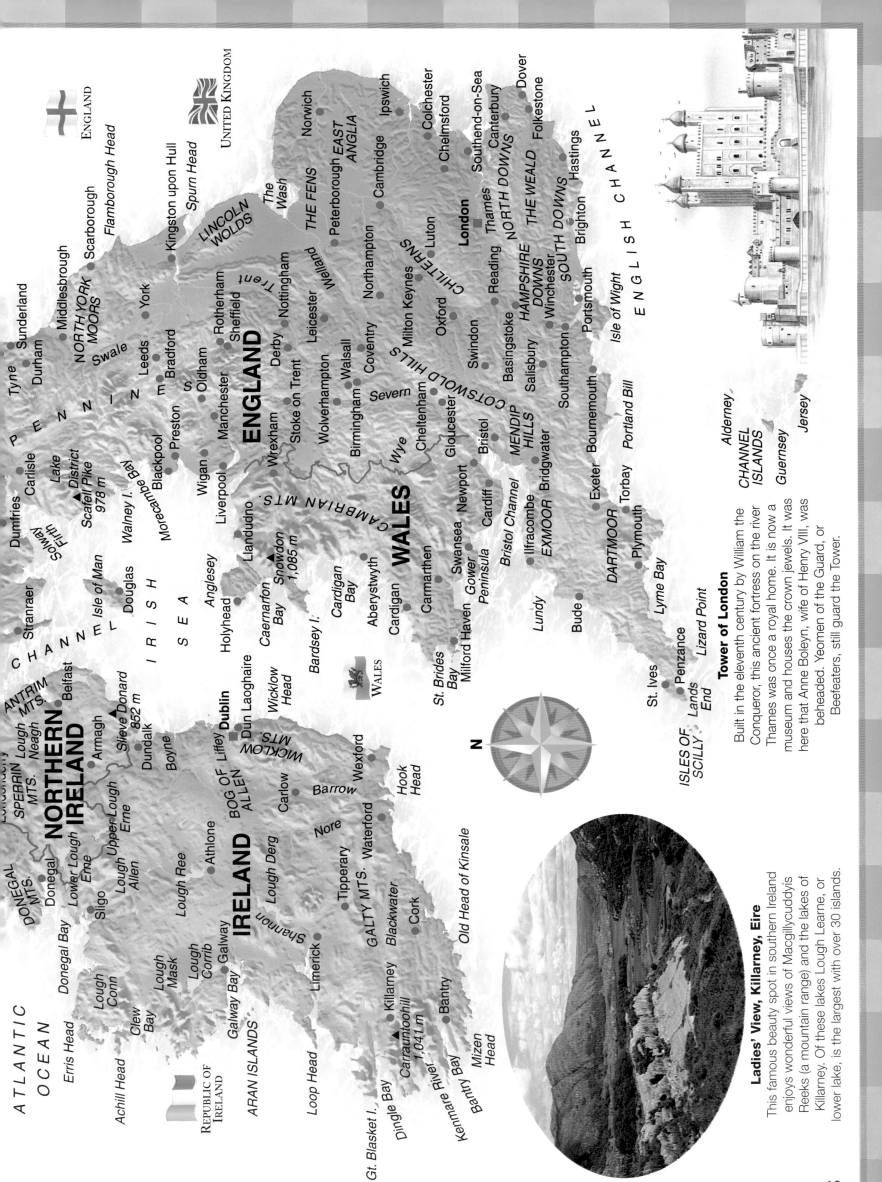

ENGLAND

UNITED KINGDOM

ATLANTIC OCEAN

CHANNEL

REPUBLIC OF IRELAND

WALES

Tower of London

Built in the eleventh century by William the Conqueror, this ancient fortress on the river Thames was once a royal home. It is now a museum and houses the crown jewels. It was here that Anne Boleyn, wife of Henry VIII, was beheaded. Yeomen of the Guard, or Beefeaters, still guard the Tower.

Ladies' View, Killarney, Eire

This famous beauty spot in southern Ireland enjoys wonderful views of Macgillycuddyís Reeks (a mountain range) and the lakes of Killarney. Of these lakes Lough Learne, or lower lake, is the largest with over 30 islands.

Map labels:

Erris Head, Achill Head, Clew Bay, Donegal Bay, DONEGAL MTS., Donegal, Sligo, Lough Conn, Lough Mask, Lough Corrib, Galway, Galway Bay, ARAN ISLANDS, Loop Head, Gt. Blasket I., Dingle Bay, Killarney, Carrauntoohill 1,041 m, Mizen Head, Bantry, Bantry Bay, Kenmare River, Cork, Blackwater, GALTY MTS., Limerick, Shannon, Tipperary, Lough Derg, Athlone, Lough Ree, Lough Allen, Upper Lough Erne, Lower Lough Erne, SPERRIN MTS., Armagh, Dundalk, Boyne, Slieve Donard 852 m, ANTRIM MTS., Belfast, Lough Neagh, NORTHERN IRELAND, IRELAND, BOG OF ALLEN, WICKLOW MTS., Dublin, Dun Laoghaire, Liffey, Wicklow Head, Wexford, Nore, Barrow, Carlow, Waterford, Hook Head, Old Head of Kinsale

Stranraer, Dumfries, Carlisle, Solway Firth, Isle of Man, Douglas, Walney I., Morecambe Bay, Blackpool, Preston, Lake District, Scafell Pike 978 m, PENNINES, Wigan, Liverpool, Holyhead, Anglesey, Llandudno, Caernarfon Bay, Snowdon 1,085 m, CAMBRIAN MTS., Bardsey I., Cardigan Bay, Cardigan, Aberystwyth, Carmarthen, St. Brides Bay, Milford Haven, Gower Peninsula, Swansea, Newport, Cardiff, Bristol Channel, Ilfracombe, Bude, Lundy, St. Ives, Penzance, Lands End, Lizard Point, ISLES OF SCILLY

Sunderland, Tyne, Durham, Middlesbrough, Scarborough, Flamborough Head, Spurn Head, Kingston upon Hull, NORTH YORK MOORS, Swale, York, Leeds, Bradford, Oldham, Manchester, Sheffield, Rotherham, LINCOLN WOLDS, The Wash, Trent, Nottingham, Derby, Stoke on Trent, Leicester, Welland, THE FENS, Peterborough, EAST ANGLIA, Norwich, Ipswich, Cambridge, Northampton, Wrexham, WALES, Wolverhampton, Walsall, Birmingham, Coventry, Severn, Cheltenham, Gloucester, Wye, COTSWOLD HILLS, Bristol, MENDIP HILLS, EXMOOR, Bridgwater, DARTMOOR, Exeter, Plymouth, Torbay, Portland Bill, Lyme Bay, Bournemouth, Southampton, SOUTH DOWNS, Winchester, Salisbury, HAMPSHIRE DOWNS, Basingstoke, Swindon, Oxford, Milton Keynes, Luton, CHILTERNS, Reading, London, Thames, NORTH DOWNS, THE WEALD, Canterbury, Folkestone, Dover, Southend-on-Sea, Chelmsford, Colchester, Brighton, Hastings, Portsmouth, Isle of Wight, ENGLISH CHANNEL, Alderney, CHANNEL ISLANDS, Guernsey, Jersey

IRISH SEA

ENGLAND

13

FRANCE AND MONACO

FRANCE IS A LARGE, beautiful country which lies at the heart of Western Europe. Its western regions include the massive peaks of the Pyrenees, vineyards and pine forests, peaceful rivers and Atlantic shores.

The north includes the stormy headlands of Brittany, the cliffs of Normandy and the Channel ports. Rolling fertile plains are drained by the winding river Seine, over whose banks and islands sprawls the French capital. Paris is one of the world's great cities, with broad avenues, historic palaces and churches.

The west of **France** is bordered by wooded hills which rise to the high forested slopes of the Jura mountains and finally the spectacular glaciers and ridges of the Alps. The rocks of the Massif Central, shaped by ancient volcanoes, rise in central southern France, to the west of the Rhône valley. The sun-baked hills of southern France border the warm seas of the Mediterranean Sea. This coast includes the wetlands of the Camargue, the great seaport of Marseilles and the fashionable yachting marinas of Cannes.

France has played a major part in history, and the French language is now spoken in many parts of the world. The French people are mostly descended from a Celtic people called the Gauls and Germanic peoples, such as the Franks and Vikings. Within France are several other peoples with their own languages and distinct cultures, such as Bretons, Basques, Catalans, Alsatians, Corsicans and Algerians.

France is a republic belonging to the European Union (EU) and is an important industrial power, producing cars, aerospace equipment, chemicals and textiles. The country is renowned for its wines, its cheeses, and its fine cooking.

Part of the Mediterranean coast is occupied by a very small principality called **Monaco**. It has close links with its large neighbour and shares the same currency. The state is famous for its casino.

Château de Charumont
France has many historical castles, palaces and stately homes, or châteaux. Some of the finest are in the Loire valley.

Cape Corse

Bastia

CORSICA

Gulf of Sagone

Ajaccio

Bonifacio

Strait of Bonifacio

Cherbourg

Carentan

St. L

Gulf of St-Malo

Granville

Morlaix

St.-Malo

Brest

St-Brieuc

Dinan

Fougeres

Douernenez

Pontivy

Vitre

Quimper

Rennes

Lorient

Vannes

Belle-Ile

Redon

St. Nazaire

Nantes

La Roche-sur-Yon

Isle d'Yeu

Les Sables-d'Olonne

Ré I.

La Rochelle

Rochefor

Oléron I.

Royan

Pauilla

Sacré-Coeur
The gleaming domes of this church soar above the Parisian district of Montmartre, once famed as the haunt of artists and writers.

Bayonne

Biarritz

P Y

S P A I N

Shape of the future
The Futuroscope theme park and study centre, near Poitiers, is one example of France's many experimental modern buildings. This theatre looks like a huge crystal.

Vineyard harvest
Grapes are gathered at a vineyard in Alsace, on the slopes of the Vosges. Grapes, grown in many regions of France, are made into some of the world's finest wines.

Dunkerque
Calais
Boulogne
Lille
Montreuil
Arras
Douai
Valenciennes
Abbeville
Cambrai
Dieppe
St. Quentin
Hirson
Amiens
Charleville-Mézières
Montdidier

BELGIUM

LUXEMBOURG

GERMANY

FRANCE

Bay of
the Seine
Fécamp
Bolbec
Le Havre
Rouen
Beauvais
Compiègne
Reims
Verdun
Metz
Caen
Louviers
Seine
Meaux
Marne
Châlons-sur-Marne
Pont à Mousson
Lisieux
Evreux
Paris
St. Dizier
Toul
Nancy
Strasbourg
Argentan
St. Germain-en-Laye
Versailles
Rambouillet
Chartres
Fontainebleau
Seine
Troyes
Epinal
Colmar
Mayenne
Nemours
Sens
Langres
Saône
Mulhouse
Laval
Orléans
Montargis
Auxerre
LANGRES PLATEAU
Montbéliard
Le Mans
Gien
Avallon
Dijon
Besançon
Doubs
Angers
Blois
Dôle
Tours
Vierzon
Loire
Autun
Pontarlier
Saumur
Bourges
Nevers
Le Creusot
Chalon-sur-Saône
Châtellerault
Cher
Châteauroux
La Châtre
Montceau les Mines
St.Claude
Poitiers
Moulins
Mâcon
Niort
Montluçon
Bourg-en-Bresse
Annecy
Civray
F R A N C E
Vichy
Villefranches
Chamonix
Cognac
Limoges
Lyon
Villeurbanne
Mont Blanc
4,807m
Angoulême
Clermont-Ferrand
Villefranches
Chambéry
Nontron
Puy de Sancy
1,886m
St.-Étienne
Vienne
Val d'Isère
Barbezieux
MASSIF
CENTRAL
Annonay
Grenoble
Périgueux
Romans-sur-Isère
Libourne
Souillac
Aurillac
Valence
Bergerac
Cère
Prives
Bordeaux
Dordogne
Gap
Marmande
Lot
Lot
Mende
Montélimar
Cahors
Rodez
Aveyron
Alès
Carpentras
LES
LANDES
Agen
Garonne
Millau
CÉVENNES
Avignon
Durance
Monte-de-Marsan
Montauban
Tarn
Gaillac
Albi
Nîmes
Nice
MONACO
Adour
Auch
Toulouse
Arles
Aix-en-Provence
Cannes
Pau
Castres
Montpellier
St.Raphael
Tarbes
Sète
Marseille
Brignoles
St.Tropez
Lourdes
St. Gaudens
Carcassonne
Béziers
Toulon
Côte d'Azur
Foix
Narbonne
Perpignan

ANDORRA

NORMANDY HILLS
Alençon
Loire
Gironde
Cère
Garonne
Ariège
Aude
PYRENEES
MONACO
SWITZERLAND
ITALY
VOSGES
JURA
Moselle
Rhine
Rhône
Isère
Drac
Durance
Verdon
ALPS
LANGUEDOC

N

Quiche Lorraine
A speciality of north-eastern
France, this is a baked pastry
tart filled with eggs, cream,
cheese and bacon.

NORTH SEA
BALTIC SEA

Sylt
Flensburg
Schleswig
Kiel Bay
Fehmarn
Rügen
Helgoland
Kiel
Mecklenburg Bay
Stralsund
Rendsburg
Neumünster
Rostock
Cuxhaven
Itzehoe
Lübeck
Wismar
Güstrow
Elmshorn
Norderstedt
Schwerin
Neubrandenburg
Wilhelmshaven
Bremerhaven
Hamburg
Emden
Buxtehude
Müritz Lake
Neustrelitz
Papenburg
Oldenburg
Bremen
Lüneburg
Uelzen
Wittenberge
Eberswalde-Finow
Delmenhorst
Weser
Elbe
Oder
Vechta
Nienburg
Celle
Stendal
Berlin
Nordhorn
Weser
Hannover
Aller
Wolfsburg
Brandenburg
Potsdam
Frankfurt (an der Oder)
Rheine
Osnabrück
Minden
Hildesheim
Brunswick (Braunschweig)
Magdeburg
Eisenhüttenstadt
Gronau
TEUTOBURG FOREST
Bielefeld
Hameln
Salzgitter
Bad Harzburg
Halberstadt
Dessau
Cottbus
Neisse
Münster
Holzminden
Leine
HARZ MTS.
Bocholt
Paderborn
Göttingen
Halle
Hoyerswerda
Hamm
Nordhausen
Leipzig
Duisburg
Dortmund
Kassel
Münden
GERMANY
Meissen
Krefeld
Essen
Arnsberg
Görlitz
Mönchen-Gladbach
Wuppertal
Mühlhausen
Weimar
Dresden
Düsseldorf
Remscheid
Marburg
Erfurt
Jena
Gera
Freiberg
Solingen
Bergisch-Gladbach
THURINGIAN FOREST
Chemnitz
Cologne (Köln)
Zwickau
Aachen
Bonn
Siegen
Alsfeld
Werra
Plauen
Neuwied
Fulda
Suhl
Hof
Giessen
Fulda
Main
Daun
Koblenz
Coburg
LUXEMBOURG
Wiesbaden
Frankfurt am Main
Schweinfurt
Bayreuth
CZECH REPUBLIC
Rhine
Offenbach
Mainz
Würzburg
Bamberg
Trier
Mosel
Darmstadt
Main
STEIGERWALD
HUNSRÜCK
Worms
Kitzingen
BOHEMIAN FOREST
Saar
Ludwigshafen
Mannheim
Jagst
Fürth
Nuremberg (Nürnberg)
Kaiserslautern
Heidelberg
Saarbrücken
Karlsruhe
Heilbronn
Regensburg
Pforzheim
Passau
Baden-Baden
Stuttgart
Aalen
Ingolstadt
FRANCE
BLACK FOREST
Neckar
Tübingen
Danube
Linz
Reutlingen
SWABIAN JURA
Ulm
Augsburg
Braunau
Freiburg
Rhine
Inn
Wels
Steyr
Memmingen
Lech
Munich (München)
Gmunden
Schaffhausen
Konstanz
Kempten
Rosenheim
Salzburg
Salzach
Hallein
Basel
Winterthur
Lake Constance (Bodensee)
St Gallen
Kufstein
AUSTRIA
Baden
Zurich
Enns
Solothurn
LIECHTENSTEIN
Zugspitze 2,963 m
Kitzbühel
Neuchâtel
Lucerne
Zug
Vaduz
Innsbruck
NIEDERE TAUERN
Bern
Brenner
HOHE TAUERN
Mur
Lake Neuchâtel
SWITZERLAND
Grossglockner 2,863 m
Wolfsberg
Fribourg
Thun
Chur
Davos
ITALY
Klagenfurt
Lausanne
Interlaken
Andermatt
Villach
Drava
Lake Geneva
BERNESE ALPS
St Moritz
SLOVENIA
Montreux
LEPONTINE ALPS
Locarno
Thonon
Bellinzona
Geneva
Martigny
Zermatt
Matterhorn 4,478 m
Monte Rosa 4,634 m
Lugano

BELGIUM
POLAND

GERMANY & THE ALPS

GERMANY LIES BETWEEN Western and Central Europe. In the south the high peaks of the Alps are flanked by belts of forest.

The rolling hills and heathland of the centre stretch to the North Sea, while in the west the rivers Rhine and Moselle wind through steep valleys planted with vines. In the northeast a vast plain is bordered by the Baltic Sea and by the rivers Oder and Neisse.

For most of its history Germany has been divided into different states. Today's united Germany dates from 1990. Germany is a federal republic, which means that its regions or Länder have considerable powers. The country is a leading member of the European Union and is a major world producer of cars, electrical and household goods, medicines, chemicals, wines and beers.

Switzerland is a small country set amongst the lakes and snowy peaks of the Alps and the Jura ranges. Its beautiful landscape and historical towns attract many tourists. Industries include dairy produce, precision instruments and finance. Zurich is a world centre of banking, while Geneva is the headquarters of many international agencies, such as the Red Cross and the World Health Organization.

To the east, the tiny country of **Liechtenstein** is closely linked with Switzerland and uses the same currency. The land of **Austria** descends from the soaring peaks of the Alps to the flat lands of the Danube river valley. Austria once ruled a large empire which stretched eastwards into Hungary and southwards into Italy. Today Austria still plays an important part in Europe, making its living from tourism, farming, forestry and manufacture.

German is spoken through most of the region, with a great variety of dialects. In parts of Switzerland there are people who speak French, Italian and Romansh.

Edelweiss
This small herb, with its pretty white flower, grows in the European Alps. High mountain meadows are filled with wildflowers in spring and summer.

Brimming with beer
Munich, capital of Bavaria in southern Germany, hosts a famous beer festival every October. Regional dress is still common in the region.

River of ice
This impressive glacier grinds its way down the Alps near Zermatt. Many tourists and climbers visit Switzerland to enjoy the spectacular views.

Medieval revelry
Festival costumes recall the Middle Ages in Baden Württemberg. During that period Germany was made up of many small states.

Krems
Danube **Vienna**
St Pölten
Baden   Bruck
Wiener Neustadt   *Neusiedler See*
Kapfenberg
Leeben
Graz
HUNGARY

IBERIAN PENINSULA

THE IBERIAN PENINSULA is in southwestern Europe, and juts out into the Atlantic Ocean. It is bordered to the north by the stormy Bay of Biscay and to the south by the Mediterranean Sea and the Balearic Islands. Across the Strait of Gibraltar, just 13 kilometres away, lies the continent of Africa.

The north coast, green from high rainfall, rises to the Cantabrian mountains, while the snowy Pyrenees form a high barrier along the Spanish-French frontier. Another range, the Sierra Nevada, runs parallel with the south coast. Inland, much of the Iberian peninsula is taken up by an extremely dry, rocky plateau, which swelters in the heat of summer. To the west are forested highlands and the fertile plains of Portugal, crossed by great rivers such as the Douro, Tagus and Guadiana.

The Iberian peninsula is occupied by four countries or territories. There is **Gibraltar**, a British colony since 1713, and the tiny independent state of **Andorra**, high in the Pyrenees. The two main countries of the region are **Spain** and **Portugal**. Both have a history of overseas settlement, and both Spanish and Portuguese have become the chief languages of Latin America. Many people speak other languages, including Basque and Catalan, and have their own traditions and history.

Both Spain and Portugal were ruled by dictators for much of the 20th century, but today both are democracies and members of the European Union. Spain produces olives, citrus fruits, wines and sherries, and has a large fishing fleet. Portugal also produces wine and port takes its name from the city of Oporto. Fishing villages line the coasts and cork, used for bottle stoppers and tiling, is cut from the thick bark of the cork oak tree.

PORTUGAL

Feria in Seville
At the Feria, held in the Spanish city of Seville every April, people ride into town dressed in traditional finery. The river is lined with tents and pavilions. The festival is celebrated with bullfights, flamenco music and dancing.

Fishing boats, Nazaré
Fishing boats line the beach at Nazaré, on the Portuguese coast. The fishermen brave the Atlantic waves daily in their search for the sardines and tuna that make up their catch.

FACT BOX

◆ **Spain**
Area: 504,880 sq km
Population: 39,300,000
Capital: Madrid
Official language: Spanish
Currency: Peseta

◆ **Portugal**
Area: 91,630 sq km
Population: 9,900,000
Capital: Lisbon
Official language: Portuguese
Currency: Escudo

◆ **Andorra**
Area: 465 sq km
Population: 62,000
Capital: Andorra la Vella
Official language: Catalan
Currency: French franc, Spanish peseta

Santander
San Sebastián
Bilbao
MOUNTAINS
Reinosa
Vitoria
Pamplona
FRANCE
PYRENEES
ANDORRA
Pico de Aneto 3,404m
Andorra la Vella
Osorno
Logroño
Arga
Ebro
Gállego
Cinca
Llobregat
Figueras
Burgos
Palencia
Soria
Ebro
Gerona
Manresa
Costa Brava
Duero
Saragossa
Lérida
Tarrasa
SPAIN
Jalón
Caspe
Reus
Barcelona
Segovia
SIERRA DE GUADARRAMA
Tajuña
Tajo
Morella
Vinaroz
Tarragona
Tortosa
Costa Dorada
Cape Tortosa
Guadalajara
Alcalá de Henares
Teruel
Mijares
Castellón de la Plana
Costa del Azahar
Madrid
Cuenca
Turia
Sagunto
SPAIN
Menorca
Mallorca
Mahón
Aranjuez
Requena
Valencia
Palma
Manacor
Toledo
Júcar
Alcira
Gulf of Valencia
BALEARIC ISLANDS
MONTES DE TOLEDO
Villarrobledo
Albacete
Almansa
Cape Neo
Ibiza
Ibiza
Formentera
Daimiel
Manzanares
Alcaraz
Alcoy
Guadiana
Ciudad Real
Yecla
Puertollano
Valdepeñas
SIERRA DE SEGURA
Segura
Alicante
Elche
Costa Blanca
MORENA
La Carolina
Moratalla
Orihuela
Linares
Cehegín
Murcia
Jaén
Cartagena
Cape Palos
Martos
Lorca
Cape Neo
Baza
Aguilas
Guadix
Huércal Overa
Costa Blanca
Genil
Granada
Mulhacén 3,478m
Antequera
SIERRA NEVADA
Almería
Cape Gata
Málaga
Motril
Berja
Costa del Sol
MEDITERRANEAN SEA

ANDORRA

SPAIN

Portuguese explorers
This monument is in Lisbon, the Portuguese capital. It honours the Portuguese seafarers who were among the first Europeans to explore the coasts of Africa, Asia and the Americas. Prince Henry (1394–1460) founded the first school of navigation.

Spanish paella
Paella takes its name from the large pan in which it is cooked. It is made of rice with saffron and garlic, mixed with prawns and other seafoods, vegetables, chicken or ham.

Melilla (Spain)

ITALY AND ITS NEIGHBOURS

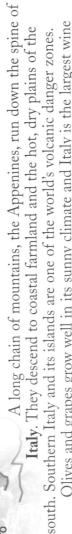

ITALY OCCUPIES a long, boot-shaped peninsula which stretches south from the snowy peaks and blue lakes of the Alps into the Mediterranean Sea. The country also takes in the large islands of Sardinia and Sicily. The northern regions of the mainland include the wide, fertile plains around the river Po and wealthy industrial cities.

A long chain of mountains, the Appenines, run down the spine of Italy. They descend to coastal farmland and the hot, dry plains of the south. Southern Italy and its islands are one of the world's volcanic danger zones. Olives and grapes grow well in its sunny climate and Italy is the largest wine producer in the world. Factories produce cars, textiles and leather goods.

Modern Italy has only been united since 1861, but in ancient times Rome was the capital of a vast empire which stretched across western Europe, southwest Asia and North Africa. Rome later became the centre of the Catholic Church and during the 1400s and 1500s cities such as Florence saw a great flowering of scholarship and the arts, known as the Renaissance. Many tourists visit Italy to see its ancient sites.

Italian, based on the ancient Latin language, is spoken throughout Italy, but in border regions you may hear other languages – French, German or Slovenian. The Ladin language is spoken in the Dolomite mountains and the people of Sardinia speak their own ancient dialect of Italian.

Two small independent states lie entirely surrounded by Italian territory. One is the world's smallest country, known as **Vatican City**. It is a district of Rome which serves as headquarters for the Pope and the Roman Catholic Church. The other is the tiny **San Marino.**

South of Italy, towards the coast of North Africa is the chain of islands which make up **Malta.** The Maltese have their own language and live from building and repairing ships and from tourism.

Sun and sea

Portofino is a small town on the Gulf of Genoa, in Italy's Liguria region. Its pretty waterfront and fishing boats attract many tourists in the hot Mediterranean summer.

Spaghetti Bolognese

Spaghetti is a kind of pasta. Made from wheat and eggs, pasta is eaten in all kinds of shapes and sizes, each with its own name. Here it is served with a meat and tomato sauce, invented in the city of Bologna. Italians who have left their homeland have made their cooking popular around the world.

Map labels:

SLOVENIA
AUSTRIA
SWITZERLAND
FRANCE
ITALY
LIGURIAN SEA
Gulf of Genoa
VATICAN CITY
MONACO
SAN MARINO

Mont Blanc 4,807m
Monte Rosa 4,634m
Biella
Turin
Cuneo
Alessandra
Novi Ligure
Savona
Genoa
La Spezia
Massa
Carrara
Viareggio
Lucca
Pisa
Livorno
Piombino
Elba
Capraia
Grosseto
L. Bolsena
Perugia
L. Trasimeno
Cortona
Arezzo
Siena
Florence
Pistoia
Bologna
Modena
Reggio nell'Emilia
Parma
Piacenza
Lodi
Cremona
Pavia
Milan
Monza
Bergamo
Lecco
L. Como
L. Maggiore
Trento
Bolzano
Borgo
Trieste
Udine
Portogruaro
Venice
Treviso
Vicenza
Padua
Verona
L. Garda
Mantova
Carpi
Ferrara
Adria
Chioggia
Comacchio
Ravenna
Forlì
Rimini
Pesaro
San Marino
Ancona
Iesi
Macerata
Gubbio
Teramo
San Benedetto
Terni
Novi Ligure
Oglio
Ticino
Tanaro
Po
Piave
Reno
Panaro
Arno

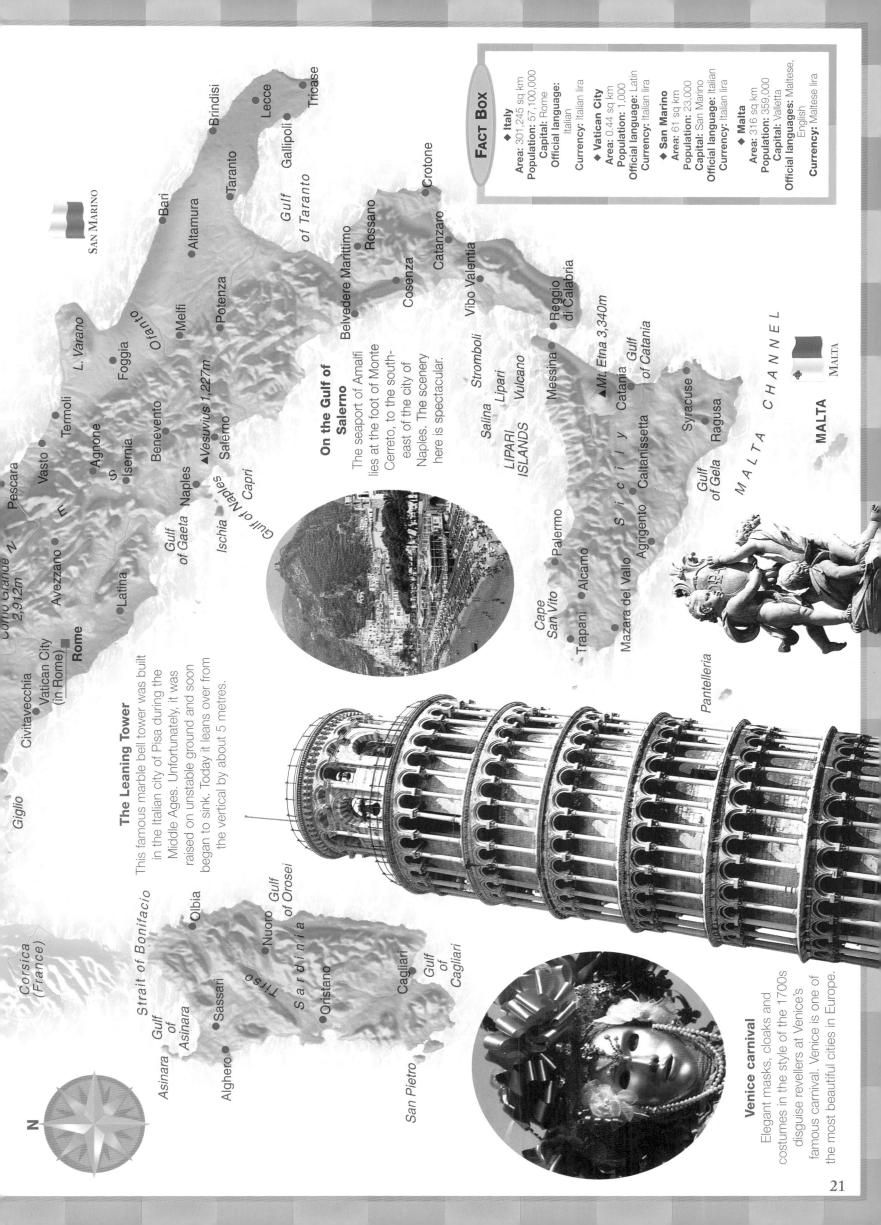

SAN MARINO

Tricase
Lecce
Gallipoli
Brindisi
Taranto
Gulf of Taranto
Bari
Altamura
Belvedere Marittimo
Rossano
Crotone
Catanzaro
Cosenza
Vibo Valentia
Reggio di Calabria
Messina
Stromboli
Lipari
Vulcano
Salina
LIPARI ISLANDS
Mt. Etna 3,340m
Catania
Gulf of Catania
S i c i l y
Syracuse
Ragusa
Caltanissetta
Gulf of Gela
Agrigento
Palermo
Alcamo
Trapani
Cape San Vito
Mazara del Vallo
Pantelleria

MALTA CHANNEL
MALTA

On the Gulf of Salerno

The seaport of Amalfi lies at the foot of Monte Cerreto, to the south-east of the city of Naples. The scenery here is spectacular.

Pescara
Vasto
Termoli
Agnone
Isernia
Benevento
Melfi
Potenza
Foggia
L. Varano
Ofanto
▲Vesuvius 1,227m
Salerno
Naples
Gulf of Gaeta
Capri
Ischia
Gulf of Naples
Latina
Avezzano
Corno Grande 2,912m
Rome
Vatican City (in Rome)
Civitavecchia
Giglio

The Leaning Tower

This famous marble bell tower was built in the Italian city of Pisa during the Middle Ages. Unfortunately, it was raised on unstable ground and soon began to sink. Today it leans over from the vertical by about 5 metres.

Corsica (France)
Strait of Bonifacio
Asinara
Gulf of Asinara
Sassari
Alghero
Olbia
Nuoro
Gulf of Orosei
Tirso
S a r d i n i a
Oristano
Cagliari
Gulf of Cagliari
San Pietro

Venice carnival

Elegant masks, cloaks and costumes in the style of the 1700s disguise revellers at Venice's famous carnival. Venice is one of the most beautiful cities in Europe.

N

CENTRAL EUROPE

THREE SMALL COUNTRIES cluster around the eastern shores of the Baltic Sea. **Estonia**, **Latvia** and **Lithuania** were part of the Soviet Union (today's Russian Federation) from 1940 until 1991, when they became independent. Their lands include forests and lakes, farmland and industrial cities.

Poland, which has historic links with Lithuania, is a large country which has also known invasions and foreign rule through much of its history. Despite this, the Poles, a Slavic people, have kept a sense of independence and a pride in their traditions. The lands near Poland's Baltic coast are dotted with lakes. The north is a flat land of pine forests, part of the great plain which stretches from eastern Germany into Russia. It is cold and snowy in winter, but warm in summer. In southern Poland the land rises to highlands and the jagged peaks of the Tatra mountains, along the Slovakian border.

Slovakia and the **Czech Republic** were a single country until 1993. Slovakia is a land of high mountains dropping to fertile farmland around the River Danube, which forms its southeastern border. When the two countries divided, most industry lay on the Czech side of the border. The Czech Republic produces beer, glass, ceramics, steel and machinery. The country is bordered by mountains and, in the east, by the Bohemian centre of learning and the arts.

The Czechs and Slovaks are both Slavic peoples, but the Hungarians are Magyars, a people who invaded and settled in the region about 1200 years ago. **Hungary** is a country of wide open plains and low mountains. Its fertile farmland produces fruits, grains and grapes for making strong red wine. Its beautiful capital, Budapest, is on the River Danube.

Historical Prague
Prague, capital of the Czech Republic, is a fine old city on the River Vltava. Prague was the chief city of independent Bohemia in the Middle Ages.

Fact Box

◆ **Poland**
Area: 312,685 sq km
Population: 38,600,000
Capital: Warsaw
Official language: Polish
Currency: Zloty

◆ **Czech Republic**
Area: 78,864 sq km
Population: 10,330,000
Capital: Prague
Official language: Czech
Currency: Koruna

◆ **Slovakia**
Area: 49,035 sq km
Population: 5,400,000
Capital: Bratislava
Official language: Slovak
Currency: Koruna

◆ **Hungrary**
Area: 93,034 sq km
Population: 10,294,000
Capital: Budapest
Official language: Hungarian
Currency: Forint

◆ **Latvia**
Area: 63,700 sq km
Population: 2,700,000
Capital: Riga
Official language: Latvian
Currency: Lats

◆ **Lithuania**
Area: 65,200 sq km
Population: 3,742,000
Capital: Kiev
Official language: Vilnius
Currency: Litas

◆ **Estonia**
Area: 45,100 sq km
Population: 1,517,000
Capital: Tallinn
Official language: Estonian
Currency: Kroon

ESTONIA
LATVIA
LITHUANIA
POLAND

RUSSIA

Lake Peipus

Kohtla-Järve
Tartu
Munamagi 318 m

E S T O N I A
Parnu
Tallinn

Hiumaa
Saaremaa

Gulf of Riga

L A T V I A
Gaizina 311 m
Daugavpils

Ventspils
Jurmala
Riga
Jelgava
Saldus
Liepāja

Utena
Panevezys
Siauliai

L I T H U A N I A
Ukmerge
Vilnius *311 m*
Kaunas

Nemunas (Neman)
Klaipeda

Kaliningrad (RUSSIA)
Kaliningrad

Gulf of Gdansk
Gdansk
Gdynia

N

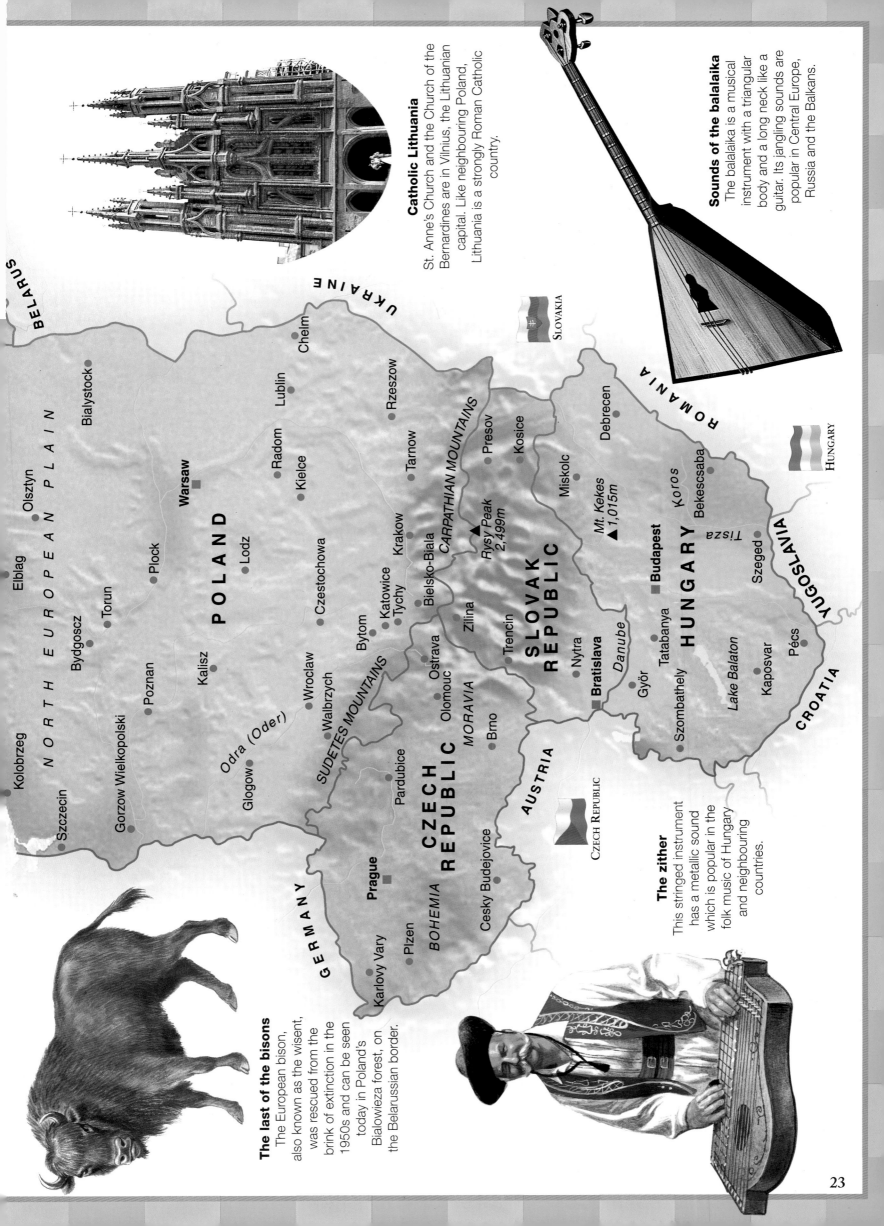

Sounds of the balalaika
The balalaika is a musical instrument with a triangular body and a long neck like a guitar. Its jangling sounds are popular in Central Europe, Russia and the Balkans.

Catholic Lithuania
St. Anne's Church and the Church of the Bernardines are in Vilnius, the Lithuanian capital. Like neighbouring Poland, Lithuania is a strongly Roman Catholic country.

BELARUS

UKRAINE

SLOVAKIA

ROMANIA

HUNGARY

Chelm

Lublin

Rzeszow

N O R T H   E U R O P E A N   P L A I N

Bialystock

Radom

Tarnow

Presov

Kosice

Debrecen

Olsztyn

Elblag

Warsaw

Kielce

Krakow

CARPATHIAN MOUNTAINS

Rysy Peak
2,499m

Miskolc

Bekescsaba

Koros

P O L A N D

Plock

Lodz

Czestochowa

Bielsko-Biala

Zilina

Mt. Kekes
▲ 1,015m

Tisza

Szeged

YUGOSLAVIA

Kolobrzeg

Poznan

Kalisz

Katowice
Tychy

Bytom

Trencin

S L O V A K
R E P U B L I C

Nytra

Budapest

H U N G A R Y

Pécs

Gorzow Wielkopolski

Wroclaw

Walbrzych

SUDETES MOUNTAINS

MORAVIA

Brno

Danube

Bratislava

Györ

Tatabanya

Lake Balaton

Kaposvar

CROATIA

Szczecin

Glogow

Odra (Oder)

Pardubice

C Z E C H
R E P U B L I C

Ostrava
Olomouc

AUSTRIA

Szombathely

Bydgoscz

Torun

Karlovy Vary

Plzen

Prague

Cesky Budejovice

BOHEMIA

G E R M A N Y

CZECH REPUBLIC

The last of the bisons
The European bison, also known as the wisent, was rescued from the brink of extinction in the 1950s and can be seen today in Poland's Bialowieza forest, on the Belarussian border.

The zither
This stringed instrument has a metallic sound which is popular in the folk music of Hungary and neighbouring countries.

23

BALKANS AND ROMANIA

THE STATES OF SOUTHERN Central Europe are known as the Balkans. They take their name from the Balkan peninsula, a great wedge of land which stretches south into the Mediterranean.

The warm, blue waters around the Balkan coast form the Adriatic, Aegean and Black Seas and are popular with tourists. The region is mountainous, with hot, dry summers. Winters are severe in the north of the region, but generally mild in the south. Earthquakes are common. The Balkan countries produce fruit, wines and spirits, dairy products such as yoghurt and cheese, olives, sunflowers and tobacco.

In the early 1990s the northwest of the region saw bitter fighting as the large nation of Yugoslavia broke up into separate independent states. These took the names of **Slovenia**, **Croatia**, **Bosnia-Herzegovina**, **Yugoslavia** (Serbia and Montenegro), and **Macedonia** (which is also the name of the northernmost province of Greece). The small and very poor country of **Albania** also suffered from political unrest and civil war in the 1990s.

The northeast of the Balkan peninsula is occupied by **Bulgaria**, a land of fertile farmland to the south of the river Danube, crossed by the Balkan and Rhodope mountain chains. Its northern neighbour is **Romania**, lying around the forested Carpathian mountain range and the Transylvanian Alps. On the Black Sea coast, the river Danube forms a marshy delta region.

The Balkan peninsula narrows to the south, breaking up into the headland of the Peloponnese and scattered island chains. **Greece** was the centre of Europe's first great civilizations, between 4,000 and 2,000 years ago. The rock of the Acropolis, with its temple, the Parthenon, still towers above the Greek capital, Athens.

Off to market
Romanian farmers gather for a cattle fair at Sugatag. The population as a whole is made up of Romanians, whose language is linked to the Latin language of the ancient Roman empire, as well as Magyars and Gypsies.

The sunflower crop
Sunflowers are grown in many parts of southern Europe. Their seeds may be roasted and eaten as snacks, turned into cooking oil or used to make margarine.

Old-fashioned style
Traditional Bulgarian costumes, with waistcoats, aprons and skirts may still be seen at many festivals or folk dances.

SLOVENIA

CROATIA

BOSNIA-
HERZEGOVINA

N

AUSTRIA

Triglav 2,863 m
Ljubljana
Maribor
Koprivnica
SLOVENIA
Zagreb
Rijeka
Kupa
Drava
CROATIA
Sava
Pula
Prijedor
Cres
Bihac
Banja Luka
Losinj
Gospic
BOSNIA -
HERZEGOVINA
Zadar
Zenica
Dugi I.
Livno
Sarajevo
Sibenik
DINARIC
Split
Brac
Mostar
Hvar
Vis
ALPS
Korcula
Lastovo
Mljet
Dubrovnik

UKRAINE

MOLDOVA

ROMANIA

ROMANIA

Satu Mare
Baia Mare
Somes
Oradea
Cluj-Napoca
Mures
Tîrgu Mures
Botosani
Iasi
Bacau

MOLDAVIAN CARPATHIANS

Siret

HUNGARY

Arad
Mures
Alba Iulia
Deva
Sibiu
Brasov
Galati
R O M A N I A
Timisoara
Moldoveanu
▲ *2,543 m*
TRANSYLVANIAN ALPS
Braila

Tisza
Subotica
Osijek
VOJVODINA
Novi Sad
Resita
Jiu
Ploiesti

Brcko
Belgrade
Smederevo
Pitesti
Bucharest
DOBRUJA

Tuzla
Sabac
Negotin
Vidin
Dunarea (Danube)
Ruse
Constanta

Srebrenica
Valjevo
Kragujevac
Mikhaylovgrad
Iskur
Pleven
Dobrich
Balchik

Drina
Cacak
Morava
Vratsa
Lovech
Turgovishte
Kamchiya
Varna

Novi Pazar
SERBIA
Nis
BALKAN MOUNTAINS
Sofia
Kazanluk
Sliven
Burgas

MONTENEGRO
Pristina
Leskovac
BULGARIA
Tundzha Yambol

Podgorica
Pec
KOSOVO
Urosevac
Musala Peak
Pasardzhik
Stara Zagora

Lake Scutari
Pernik
▲ *2,925 m*
Maritsa
Plovdiv
Khaskovo

hkodèr
Skopje
Tetovo
Smolyan
Orestiás

Drin Gulf
Mt Korabit ▲
2,751 m
RHODOPE MOUNTAINS
Komotini

Durrës
MACEDONIA
Prilep
Drama
Xánthi

Elbasan
Lake Ohrid
Bitola
Palikastron
Sérrai
Kaválla
Alexandroúpolis

Lake Prespa
Edhessa
Kilkís

ALBANIA
Náousa
Thásos
Samothrace

Vlore
Ptolemais
Thessaloníki

Gjirokaster
Aliákmon
Mt Olympus
▲ *2,917 m*
Mt Athos
2,033 m
Límnos

GREECE
Ioánnina
Trikkala
Lárisa
Mitilíni
Lesbos

Kérkira
Corfu
Párga
PINDUS MTS
Vólos
Skíathos
Skíros

Arta
Kardhítsa
Skópelos
Chios

Pálairos
Leukas
Lamia
Euboea
Kími

Astakós
Agrínion
Parnassus
▲ *2,547 m*
Khalkís
A E G E A N   S E A
Chios

Cephalonia
Ithaca
Pátrai
Mégara
Marathon
Ándros
Sámos

I O N I A N   S E A
Lambía
Corinth
Piraeus
Tínos
Ikaría

Amaliás
Argos
Athens
Kéa

Zante
Pírgos
Alfíos
Láyrion
Kíthnos
Síros
Míkonos
Pátmos

Trípolis
Návplion
Galatás
Sérifos
Páros
Léros

Kalamáta
P E L O P O N N E S U S
Sparta
Sífnos
Náxos
Kálimnos
Cos

Areópolis
Mílos
Íos
Astipálaia
Tílos
Rhodes

Neápolis
Thíra
Rhodes
Líndos

Cythera
SEA OF CRETE
Kárpathos

Khaniá
Réthimnon
Iráklion
Crete
Mt. Ida
▲ *2,456 m*

Islands from volcanoes
The Greek island of Santorini (or Thira) is one of the islands that form the Cyclades in the Aegean Sea. Once a volcano, the island has steep cliffs and narrow, winding streets. It has become a popular destination for tourists.

YUGOSLAVIA

BULGARIA

MACEDONIA

GREECE

ALBANIA

Clear waters
A waterfall sparkles in the sunshine in Croatia. This is a small country of many landscapes.

25

RUSSIA AND ITS NEIGHBOURS

FOR A LARGE PART OF THIS CENTURY all the countries on this map were part of one huge country, the Soviet Union. That nation was formed in the years after November 1917, when communists seized power from the czars. Communist rule ended in 1991 and many of the regions around the former Soviet borders then broke away to become independent countries.

St Basil's Cathedral, Russia
Moscow is famous for the onion-shaped domes of St Basil's Cathedral. It was built in 1555 by Czar Ivan IV to commemorate the defeat of invading Tartars.

The remaining part of the former Soviet Union was renamed the '**Russian Federation**'. It is still by far the largest country in the world, stretching across two continents, Europe and Asia. Eighty percent of the population are Russians, but the rest belong to one of the many other ethnic groups who live in this enormous region.

Northern Russia is a land of tundra, where deep-frozen soil borders the Arctic Ocean. To the south is the great belt of forest known as taiga, whose spruce trees are heavy with snow during the long, bitter winter. Southern Russia and the **Ukraine** have the fertile black earth of the rolling grasslands known as steppes. The lands to the south of Russia's new borders take in warm, fertile valleys, thin grasslands grazed by sheep and goats, deserts and high mountains.

Russia is rich in minerals, oil, natural gas and timber. Its industries were developed in a hurry during the Soviet years, but at great cost to its people and environment. Russia is still an economic giant, producing machinery, textiles, chemicals and vehicles.

Franz Josef Land

BELARUS
FINLAND
LITHUANIA
RUSSIA
LATVIA
ESTONIA
UKRAINE

Murmansk *BARENTS SEA*
Novaya Zemlya
KARA SEA

L. Ladoga
Archangel
Amderma
Dikson

St Petersburg
L. Onega
N. Dvina

BELARUS
Minsk
Gomel
Smolensk
Yaroslavl'
Salekhard
SIBERIAN LOWLAND

Pechora
URAL MOUNTAINS
Ob'

UKRAINE
MOLDOVA
Chisinau
Kiev
Chernobyl
Moscow
Kirov
Volga
Yenisey

Nizhniy Novgorod
Kazan
Perm
Khanty-Mansiysk

Dnepr
Voronezh
Kama
Nizhniy Tagil
Irtysh

Khar'kov
Syzran
Ufa
Tobol'sk
Ob'

Odessa
Donetsk
Saratov
Samara
Yekaterinburg
Yenisey

Sevastopol
Don
Volgograd
Volga
Magnitogorsk
Chelyabinsk

BLACK SEA
Rostov-on-Don
Ural
Orsk
Omsk
Tomsk

Mt. Elbrus
5,642 m
CAUCASUS MTS.
Astrakhan
Magnitogorsk
Novosibirsk

MOLDOVA
Batumi
Groznyy
Ishim
Aqmola
Irtysh

GEORGIA
Tbilisi
ARMENIA
Yerevan
AZERBAIJAN
AZER.
K A Z A K H S T A N
Karaganda
Semey
SAYAN

ARMENIA
Caspian Sea
Baku
Aral Sea
Syr Dar'ya
Balkhash

TURANIAN PLATEAU
Nukus
Lake Balkhash
CHINA

UZBEKISTAN
TURKMENISTAN
Ashgabat
Tashauz
UZBEKISTAN
Almaty

IRAN
Amu Darya
Bukhara
Tashkent
Bishkek
KYRGYZSTAN

AZERBAIJAN
TURKMENISTAN
Dushanbe
TAJIKISTAN
AFGHANISTAN
KYRGYZSTAN
TAJIKSTAN

Coarse cotton

Cotton of a tough, coarse grade is grown in Uzbekistan. The country is a major world producer, but in this dry land the cotton crop needs a great deal of irrigation, and this has harmed the environment.

Happy Easter!

Many Russians are Christians belonging to the Eastern Orthodox Church. Traditionally, they exchanged beautifully decorated eggs as gifts at Easter.

RUSSIA

Severnaya Zemlya

New Siberian Islands

Wrangel I.

Anadyr'

EAST SIBERIAN SEA

LAPTEV SEA

Os. Lyakhovskiy

Delta of the Lena

Nordvik

Kolyma

KOLYMA LOWLAND

Indigirka

CHERSKIY RANGE

VERKHOYANSK RANGE

KOLIMA MOUNTAINS

KAMCHATKA PENINSULA

Commander Is.

CENTRAL SIBERIAN PLATEAU

Lena

Magadan

Lower Tunguska

I A

Yakutsk

Olekminsk

Lensk

ALDAN MOUNTAINS

DZUGDZHUR

Petropavlovsk-Kamchatskiy

SEA OF OKHOTSK

Sakhalin

STANOVOY RANGE

Tatarskiy Proliv

SIKHOTE ALIN'

Angara

Yuzhno-Sakhalinsk

Bratsk

Krasnoyarsk

Lake Baykal

YABLONOVVY MOUNTAINS

Amur

Khabarovsk

CHINA

Irkutsk

Yenisey MTS.

Ulan-Ude

Vladivostok

MONGOLIA

KAZAKHSTAN

N

FACT BOX

◆ **Russia**
Area: 17,078,005 sq km
Population: 148,673,000
Capital: Moscow
Official language: Russian
Currency: Rouble

◆ **Belarus**
Area: 208,000 sq km
Population: 10,313,000
Capital: Minsk
Official language: Belarussian
Currency: Rouble

◆ **Ukraine**
Area: 603,700 sq km
Population: 52,194,000
Capital: Kiev
Official language: Ukrainian
Currency: Karbovanets

◆ **Moldova**
Area: 33,7000 sq km
Population: 4,356,000
Capital: Chisinau
Official language: Moldovan
Currency: Leu

◆ **Kazakhstan**
Area: 2,717,300 sq km
Population: 17,035,000
Capital: Almaty
Official language: Kazakh
Currency: Tenge

◆ **Armenia**
Area: 30,000 sq km
Population: 3,677,000
Capital: Yerevan
Official language: Armenian
Currencies: Dram, rouble

◆ **Georgia**
Area: 69,700 sq km
Population: 5,471,000
Capital: Tbilisi
Official language: Georgian
Currency: Lari

◆ **Azerbaijan**
Area: 87,000 sq km
Population: 7,398,000
Capital: Baku
Official language: Azeri
Currencies: Manat, rouble

◆ **Turkmenistan**
Area: 488,100 sq km
Population: 3,714,000
Capital: Ashkhabad
Official language: Turkmen
Currency: Manat

◆ **Uzbekistan**
Area: 447,400 sq km
Population: 21,207,000
Capital: Tashkent
Official language: Uzbek
Currencies: Som, rouble

◆ **Tajikstan**
Area: 143,100 sq km
Population: 5,514,000
Capital: Dushanbe
Official language: Tajik
Currency: Rouble

◆ **Kyrgyzstan**
Area: 198,500 sq km
Population: 4,528,000
Capital: Bishkek
Official language: Kyrgyz
Currency: Som

In the Caucasus

This woman wears a traditional costume of Dagostan, a part of the Russian Federation which lies between the Caucasus mountains and the Caspian Sea. About 30 different ethnic groups live in this region.

27

CANADA AND GREENLAND

FACT BOX

◆ **Canada**
Area: 9,922,385 sq km
Population: 30,000,000
Capital: Ottawa
Official languages: French, English

◆ **Greenland**
Area: 2,175,600 sq km
Population: 57,000
Capital: Nuuk (Godthåb)
Official languages: Danish, Inuktitut
Currency: Danish krone

CANADA is the second largest country in the world and yet it is home to only 30 million people. Most Canadians live in the big cities in the south, such as Toronto, Ottawa, Montréal and Vancouver.

The southern provinces take in the St Lawrence River and Seaway, the Great Lakes, the prairies along the United States border and the foggy coasts of the Atlantic and Pacific Oceans.

The severe climate makes it hard for people to live in the northern wilderness, which stretches into the **Arctic Circle**. Here, a broad belt of spruce forest gives way to bare, deep-frozen soil called tundra, and a maze of islands locked in ice.

Canada's wilderness includes rivers, lakes, coasts and forests. It is home to polar bears and seals, caribou, moose, beavers and loons. It also has valuable resources, providing timber, hydroelectric power and minerals, including oil. **Canada** is a wealthy country.

The first Canadians crossed into North America from Asia long ago, when the two continents were joined by land. They were the Native American peoples and they were followed by the Inuit people of the Arctic. Today these two groups make up only four percent of the population. About 40 percent of Canadians are descended from peoples of the British Isles, especially Scots. People of French descent make up 27 percent, and there are also many people of Eastern European and Asian descent.

Canada has two official languages, French and English. In recent years many people in the French-speaking province of Québec have campaigned to become separate from the rest of Canada.

Across the Davis Strait, **Greenland** (or Kallaalit Nunaat) is a self-governing territory of Denmark. Its peoples are descended from both Inuit and Scandinavians.

Map labels

ARCTIC OCEAN

Melville Island

Banks Island

Prince of Wales Island

BEAUFORT SEA

Victoria Island

ALASKA (U.S.A.)

Dawson

Norman Wells

Great Bear Lake

YUKON TERRITORY

Mackenzie

NORTHWEST TERRITORIES

▲ Mt. Logan 5,951 m

Whitehorse

HORN MOUNTAINS

Yellowknife

Dubawnt Lake

Liard

Great Slave Lake

Fort Resolution

Fort Smith

BRITISH COLUMBIA

CARIBOU MOUNTAINS

Lake Athabasca

Peace

CANADA

Reindeer Lake

Churchill

Prince Rupert

Peace River

Nelson

QUEEN CHARLOTTE ISLANDS

Prince George

ALBERTA

MANITOBA

Edmonton

N. Saskatchewan

Fraser

Red Deer

Prince Albert

Lake Winnipeg

Kamloops

Lake Winnipegosis

Vancouver Island

Calgary

Saskatoon

Vancouver

Medicine Hat

SASKATCHEWAN

Lake Manitoba

Victoria

S. Saskatchewan

Regina

Winnipeg

UNITED STATES OF AMERICA

Wheat Harvest

Large combine harvesters cross the Canadian prairies. These are natural grasslands which are now largely given over to wheat and cattle production. They occupy parts of Manitoba, Saskatchewan and Alberta and stretch across the border into the northern United States.

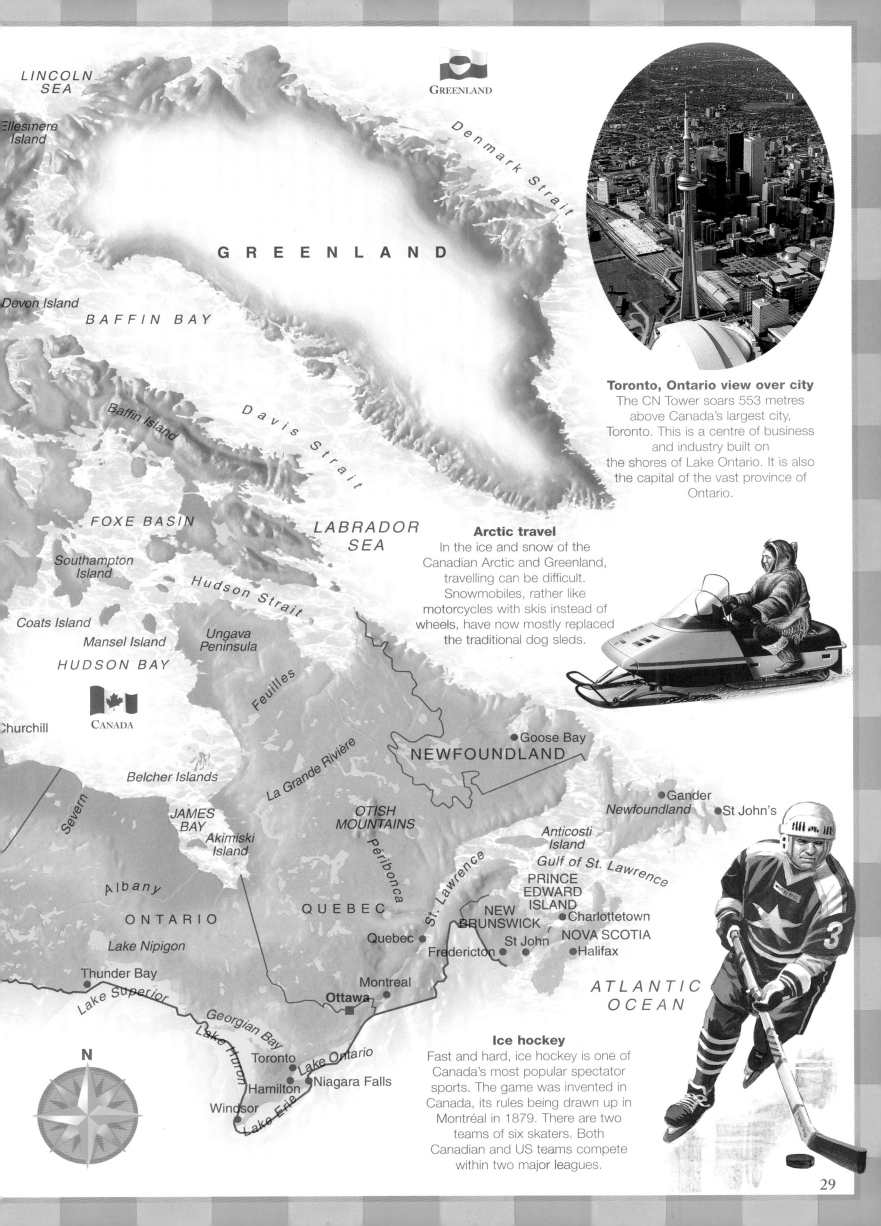

LINCOLN
SEA

Ellesmere
Island

Devon Island

BAFFIN BAY

Baffin Island

Davis Strait

Denmark Strait

GREENLAND

GREENLAND

Toronto, Ontario view over city
The CN Tower soars 553 metres
above Canada's largest city,
Toronto. This is a centre of business
and industry built on
the shores of Lake Ontario. It is also
the capital of the vast province of
Ontario.

FOXE BASIN

LABRADOR
SEA

Southampton
Island

Hudson Strait

Coats Island

Mansel Island

Ungava
Peninsula

HUDSON BAY

CANADA

Churchill

Feuilles

La Grande Rivière

Belcher Islands

Severn

JAMES
BAY

Akimiski
Island

Albany

ONTARIO

Lake Nipigon

Thunder Bay

Lake Superior

Georgian Bay

Lake Huron

N

Toronto

Hamilton

Windsor

Lake Erie

Lake Ontario

Niagara Falls

Goose Bay

NEWFOUNDLAND

OTISH
MOUNTAINS

Péribonca

QUEBEC

St. Lawrence

Quebec

Montreal

Ottawa

Gander

Newfoundland

St John's

Anticosti
Island

Gulf of St. Lawrence

PRINCE
EDWARD
ISLAND

NEW
BRUNSWICK

Charlottetown

NOVA SCOTIA

Fredericton

St John

Halifax

ATLANTIC
OCEAN

Arctic travel
In the ice and snow of the
Canadian Arctic and Greenland,
travelling can be difficult.
Snowmobiles, rather like
motorcycles with skis instead of
wheels, have now mostly replaced
the traditional dog sleds.

Ice hockey
Fast and hard, ice hockey is one of
Canada's most popular spectator
sports. The game was invented in
Canada, its rules being drawn up in
Montréal in 1879. There are two
teams of six skaters. Both
Canadian and US teams compete
within two major leagues.

USA

THE UNITED STATES OF AMERICA

make up a huge country, which crosses no less than eight time zones. It extends from the Pacific to the Atlantic Oceans, from Canada south to Mexico.

The modern nation was formed by colonists from Europe, who from the 1500s onwards seized and settled the lands of the Native American peoples. In 1776 the British colonies in the east declared their independence, and the new country grew rapidly during the 1800s as it gained territory from France, Mexico and Russia. Today, in addition to the small Native American population, there are Americans whose ancestors originally came from Britain, Ireland, Italy, France, Germany, the Netherlands and Poland. There are African Americans, whose ancestors were brought to America to work as slaves. There are Armenians, Spanish, Chinese, Cubans, Vietnamese and Koreans. All are citizens of the United States.

The nation today is a federation of 50 states, which have the power to pass many of their own laws. The federal capital is at Washington, a large city on the Potomac River, in the District of Columbia (DC). Here is the Congress, made up of a Senate and a House of Representatives, and the White House, the home of the US presidents.

The American economy is the most powerful in the world. The country is rich in minerals, including oil, coal and iron ore. American companies produce computers and software, aircraft, cars and processed foods. There are also many large banks and finance companies. America leads in space exploration and technology. The films and television programmes produced in America are watched by people in many countries around the world.

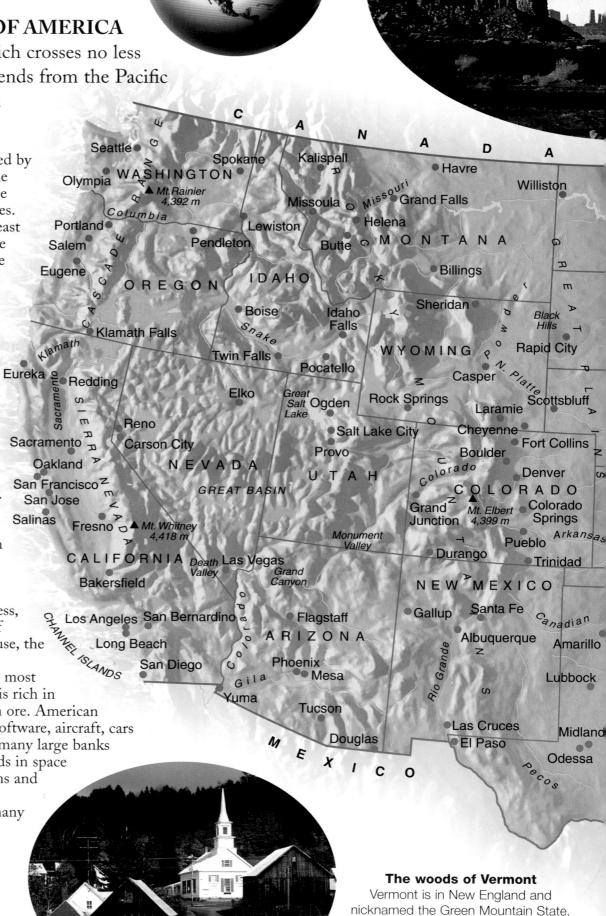

FACT BOX

◆ **United States of America**
  Area: 9,363,130 sq km
  Population: 267,700,000
  Capital: Washington DC
  Official language: English
  Currency: US dollar

The woods of Vermont
Vermont is in New England and nicknamed the Green Mountain State. It is famous for its brilliant foliage in the autumn or fall.

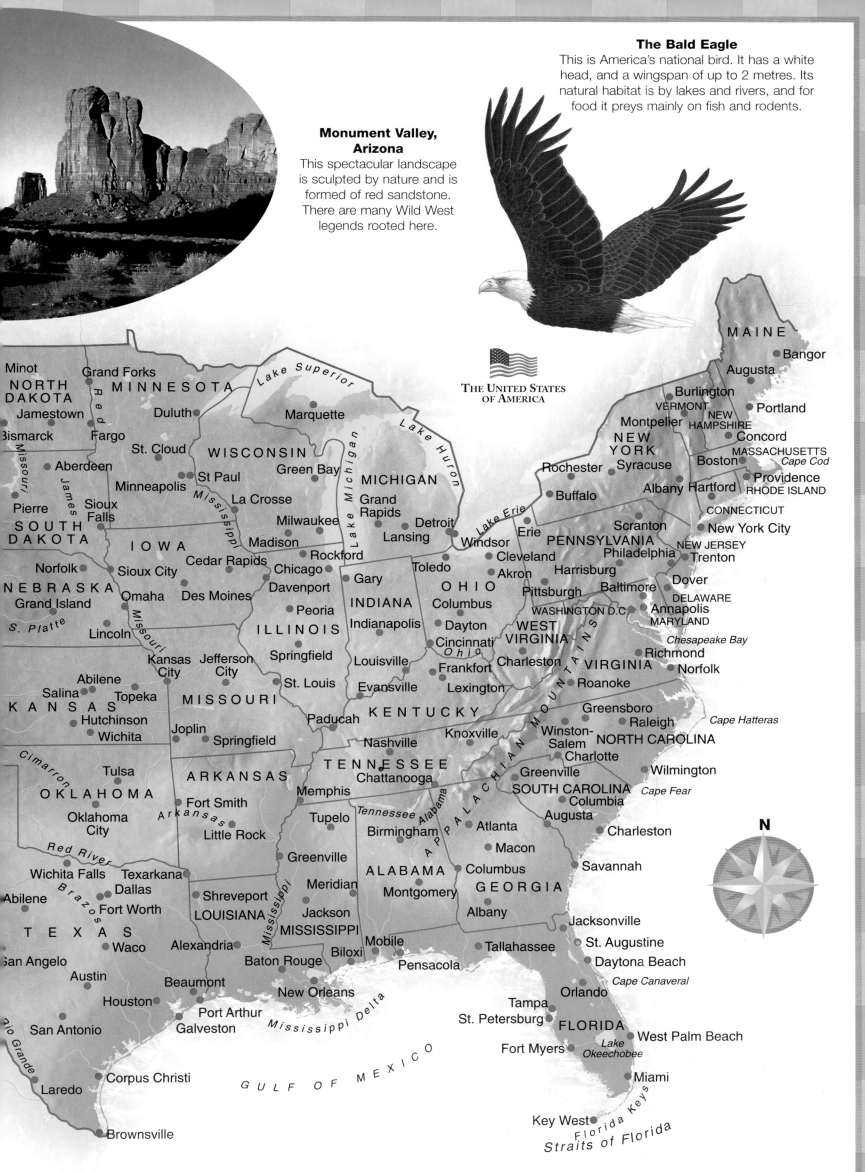

Monument Valley, Arizona

This spectacular landscape is sculpted by nature and is formed of red sandstone. There are many Wild West legends rooted here.

The Bald Eagle

This is America's national bird. It has a white head, and a wingspan of up to 2 metres. Its natural habitat is by lakes and rivers, and for food it preys mainly on fish and rodents.

THE UNITED STATES OF AMERICA

N

Minot
Grand Forks
NORTH DAKOTA
Jamestown
Bismarck
Fargo
Aberdeen
Pierre
Sioux Falls
SOUTH DAKOTA
Norfolk
Sioux City
NEBRASKA
Grand Island
Omaha
Des Moines
S. Platte
Lincoln

Duluth
MINNESOTA
Red
St. Cloud
Minneapolis
St Paul
La Crosse
WISCONSIN
Green Bay
Milwaukee
Madison
Rockford
IOWA
Cedar Rapids
Mississippi
Chicago
Davenport
Peoria
ILLINOIS
Springfield
Jefferson City
St. Louis

Lake Superior
Marquette
Lake Michigan
MICHIGAN
Grand Rapids
Lansing
Detroit

Lake Huron
Lake Erie
Windsor
Erie
Cleveland
Akron
Toledo
Gary
INDIANA
Indianapolis
Columbus
OHIO
Dayton
Cincinnati
Ohio
Louisville
Frankfort
Evansville
Lexington
KENTUCKY
Knoxville
Nashville
Paducah

MAINE
Bangor
Augusta
Burlington
VERMONT
Montpelier
NEW HAMPSHIRE
Portland
NEW YORK
Concord
Rochester
Syracuse
MASSACHUSETTS
Cape Cod
Boston
Buffalo
Albany
Hartford
Providence
RHODE ISLAND
CONNECTICUT
Scranton
New York City
PENNSYLVANIA
NEW JERSEY
Philadelphia
Trenton
Harrisburg
Pittsburgh
Baltimore
Dover
DELAWARE
WASHINGTON D.C.
Annapolis
MARYLAND
WEST VIRGINIA
Charleston
Chesapeake Bay
Richmond
VIRGINIA
Norfolk
Roanoke
Greensboro
Raleigh
Cape Hatteras
Winston-Salem
NORTH CAROLINA
Charlotte

KANSAS
Abilene
Salina
Topeka
Kansas City
Hutchinson
Wichita
Joplin
Springfield
Tulsa
Cimarron
OKLAHOMA
Oklahoma City
Fort Smith
Arkansas
Little Rock
ARKANSAS
MISSOURI

Memphis
TENNESSEE
Chattanooga
Tennessee
Alabama
Tupelo
Birmingham
APPALACHIAN MOUNTAINS
Greenville
SOUTH CAROLINA
Columbia
Augusta
Charleston
Atlanta
Macon
Savannah

Red River
Wichita Falls
Dallas
Texarkana
Fort Worth
Shreveport
LOUISIANA
Brazos
Abilene
San Angelo
Austin
TEXAS
Waco
Houston
Beaumont
Port Arthur
Galveston
San Antonio
Laredo
Corpus Christi
Brownsville
Rio Grande

Meridian
Jackson
MISSISSIPPI
Alexandria
Baton Rouge
Biloxi
Mobile
Pensacola
New Orleans
Mississippi Delta

ALABAMA
Montgomery
Columbus
GEORGIA
Albany
Tallahassee
Jacksonville
St. Augustine
Daytona Beach
Cape Canaveral
Orlando
Tampa
St. Petersburg
FLORIDA
West Palm Beach
Fort Myers
Lake Okeechobee
Miami
Key West
Florida Keys
Straits of Florida

GULF OF MEXICO

Greenville
Columbus
Wilmington
Cape Fear

The northeastern United States have a mild climate, although winter snowfall can be heavy and summers can be warm. Inland from the rocks and stormy shores of the Atlantic coast are the woodlands of the New England region, which turn to every shade of red and gold in the autumn. Here there are broad rivers and neat little towns dating back to the days of the early settlers, as well as the historic city of Boston, Massachusetts. In the far north the Great Lakes mark the border with Canada. On this border are the spectacular Niagara Falls, a major tourist attraction which also provides valuable hydroelectric power. The Appalachian mountain ranges run for 2,400 kilometres from north to south, through the eastern United States.

The northeastern United States include centres of industry and mining, and large cities with gleaming skyscrapers, sprawling suburbs, road and rail networks. New York City, centred around the island of Manhattan, is the business capital of the United States and also a lively centre of arts and entertainment. To many people, New York City is a symbol of America – fast-moving and energetic, a melting pot of different peoples and cultures. The northern city of Detroit is a centre of the motor industry, and Chicago, on the windy shores of Lake Michigan, is another bustling city of skyscrapers, and an important centre of business and manufacture.

Travelling south from the Delaware River and the great city of Philadelphia, you come to the federal District of Columbia, the site of Washington, capital city of the United States. Approaching the American South, you pass into warmer country where tobacco and cotton are grown in the red earth. The long peninsula of Florida extends southwards into the Caribbean Sea, fringed by sandy islands called keys. Along the Gulf coast the climate is hot and very humid, with creeks known as bayous and tangled swamps which are home to alligators.

Hurricanes are common in late summer and autumn. New Orleans, the home of jazz, has many picturesque old buildings with wrought-iron verandas. It lies 170 kilometres above the mouth of the Mississippi River, which together with the mighty Missouri drains the centre of the continent. Texas is a huge state which borders Mexico along the Rio Grande. Dry and dusty, it makes its living from cattle ranching and oil.

Prairies once covered the great plains of the Midwest, the home of vast herds of bison or buffalo. Today the grasslands are largely given over to farming vegetable crops and grain, or to cattle ranching. The wheat and maize produced on the Prairies have led to them being called the 'breadbasket of the world'.

Barren, stony 'badlands' rise towards the rugged Rocky Mountain ranges, which form the backbone of the United States as they stretch from the Canadian border south to Mexico. Southwards and westwards again there are large areas of burning desert, salt flats and canyons, where over the ages the rocks have been worn into fantastic shapes by wind and water. In places the Grand Canyon of Arizona is 24 kilometres wide and two kilometres deep, a spectacular gorge cut out by the waters of the Colorado River.

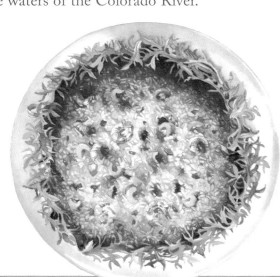

Jambalaya!
Rice, seafood, green peppers and hot spices make up this delicious dish from New Orleans, in Louisiana. The people of this city include many of French and African descent, and this shows in its cooking.

The Statue of Liberty
This huge monument, a gift from the people of France in 1886, was the first sight of America for many immigrants.

Badwater, in California's harsh Death Valley, is the lowest point in the United States, 86 metres below sea level.

The Sierra, Cascade and Coast ranges run parallel with the beautiful Pacific coast. The warm beaches, pines and gigantic redwood trees of California stretch northwards to the ferny forests of Oregon and Washington State, which is rainy and cool. Irrigation has made it possible to farm large areas of California, which produce citrus fruits and grape vines. Major cities of the west include Los Angeles, which takes in the world-famous film studios of Hollywood, beautiful San Francisco, set on a wide bay which can be warm and sparkling blue or shrouded in cool sea-fog, and the busy northern port of Seattle.

The United States has a northern outpost in oil-rich Alaska, its largest state. Alaska was purchased from Russia in 1867. Bordered by Canada, the Alaskan wilderness stretches into the remote Arctic, a deep frozen land of mountains and tundra.

Its islands are inhabited by large grizzly bears and its waters by schools of migrating whales.

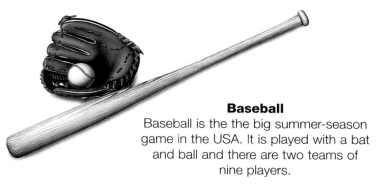

Baseball
Baseball is the the big summer-season game in the USA. It is played with a bat and ball and there are two teams of nine players.

Mount McKinley, at 6,194 metres, is the highest point not just in the United States, but in all of North America.

Far to the west, in the Pacific Ocean, the Hawaiian Islands are also part of the United States. Tourists come here to enjoy the warm climate and the surf and to see the islands' spectacular volcanoes.

The United States also governs or has special links with various other territories, such as American Samoa, the Northern Marianas and the Midway Islands in the Pacific Ocean. Puerto Rico and the US Virgin Islands in the Caribbean are also governed by the United States.

The United States has close economic links with its neighbours, Canada and Mexico, through the North American Free Trade Agreement of 1994. It is also a member of many other international groupings, such as the the North Atlantic Treaty Organization (NATO), a military alliance which links it with Western and Central Europe.

As the world's most powerful country, the influence of the United States is to be seen in many other lands. Films and television programmes have made the American way of life influential around the world. Hamburgers and soft drinks are now bought in many other countries. American blues and jazz has influenced all kinds of popular music and American slang is used by people around the world.

Manhattan
The centre of New York City is built over the island of Manhattan. Unable to build outwards, architects have built upwards. The skyline includes many famous skyscrapers. These twin towers belong to the World Trade Centre.

Cops and crime
American policemen and detectives fight city crime. Their work has been made famous around the world by countless films and television series.

Heart of the nation
The impressive Capitol building is at the centre of Washington, District of Columbia. It is used by the United States Congress and was constructed between 1851 and 1863.

Blast-off!
The space shuttle leaves Earth on another mission. The United States has been a pioneer of space exploration since the 1960s.

MEXICO, CENTRAL AMERICA & THE CARIBBEAN

Ancient stones
Many great civilizations developed in ancient times in Mexico and Central America. Statues like this, called chacmools, were used during human sacrifices.

MEXICO is a large, mountainous country with a tropical climate. It stretches southwards from the Rio Grande on the United States border, and meets the Pacific Ocean in the west and the Gulf of Mexico in the east.

Mexico is a land of deserts, forests and volcanoes, dotted with the spectacular ruins of ancient Native American civilizations, such as the Maya, Toltec and Aztec. Mexico City, built on the site of an ancient Aztec city, is a vast, sprawling centre of population.

To the south, **Central America** narrows to a thin strip of land called the isthmus of Panama. Guatemala, Belize, Honduras, El Salvador, Nicaragua, Costa Rica and Panama are all small nations that live mostly by farming tropical crops such as bananas, coffee and sugar-cane. Many Mexicans and Central Americans are of Native American, Spanish or mixed descent.

Tijuana
Mexicali
Ensenada
Cedros I.
Gulf of California
Baja California
UNITED STATES OF AMERICA
Ciudad Juárez
Rio Bravo del Norte
Rio Grande
Hermosillo
Chihuahua
SIERRA MADRE
Torreón
Monterrey
Matamoros
Culiacán
Saltillo
La Paz
Durango
SIERRA MADRE
San Luis Potosí
Tampico
Aguascalientes
Guadalajara
León
Cape Corrientes
L. de Chapala
Manzanillo
MEXICO
Mexico City
Veracruz
Puebla
Orizaba 5,700 m
Balsas
Coatzacoalcas
Acapulco
Oaxaca

GULF OF MEXICO

Havana
CUBA
CUBA
Isla de la Juventad
Yucatán Channel
Cayman Islands (U.K.)

Mérida
Cancún
Yucatán Peninsula
Bay of Campeche
Campeche
Terminos Lagoon
Villahermosa
Belize City
Belmopan
BELIZE
BELIZE

GUATEMALA
HONDURAS
Gulf of Tehuantepec
Tegucigalpa
Guatemala City
San Salvador
EL SALVADOR
NICARAGUA
Lake Nicaragua
Managua
Mosquitos Gulf
San José
COSTA RICA

PACIFIC OCEAN

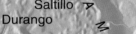
MEXICO

GUATEMALA

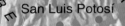
EL SALVADOR

NICARAGUA

COSTA RICA

N

Birds of a feather
The quetzal is a brilliantly coloured bird. It lives in rainforests from southern Mexico to Panama, where it feeds on berries and fruits.

Many people in Mexico and Central America are poor and the region has a long history of political strife and civil war.

The **Caribbean Sea** is part of the Atlantic Ocean and is dotted with beautiful islands in warm, blue seas. These were once home to Native American peoples such as the Arawaks and the Caribs, after whom the region is named. Then came European invaders, including the Spanish, Dutch, French and British. Most of today's Caribbeans are descended from West Africans who were brought in as slaves by the early settlers. Caribbean islanders live by fishing, farming, manufacture and tourism. Favourite sports include baseball in Cuba and cricket in Jamaica and Barbados. The region is famous for its range of popular music, from calypso to salsa, from reggae to soca.

Coconut grove
Palms line sandy beaches in the Central American republic of Costa Rica. Coconuts are common around the tropical coasts of Central America and the Caribbean.

BAHAMAS

ANTIGUA AND BARBUDA

PUERTO RICO

DOMINICA

BAHAMAS

BAHAMAS IS.

• Nassau

Andros I.

Turks & Caicos Islands (U.K.)

Virgin Is. (U.K. & U.S.)

San Juan

Puerto Rico (U.S.)

ANTIGUA & BARBUDA

Montserrat (U.K.)

Guadeloupe (FR.)

DOMINICA

Camagüey

DOMINICAN REPUBLIC

Santiago de Cuba

HAITI

Santo Domingo

Martinique (FR.)

ST. LUCIA

BARBADOS

Port-au-Prince

G R E A T E R   A N T I L L E S

Kingston

JAMAICA

C A R I B B E A N   S E A

ST. VINCENT & THE GRENADINES

GRENADA

L E S S E R   A N T I L L E S

Netherlands Antilles

TRINIDAD & TOBAGO

JAMAICA

HAITI

DOMINICAN REPUBLIC

GRENADA

HONDURAS

PANAMA

Panama City

Gulf of Panama

C O L O M B I A

ST VINCENT AND GRENADINES

TRINIDAD AND TOBAGO

ST LUCIA

BARBADOS

ST KITTS AND NEVIS

People of Panama
The Kuna are an indigenous people who live on the coasts and islands of Panama and Colombia. They mostly live by fishing and are well known for their craft work, which includes wood carving and the making of molas, the colourful blouses being worn here.

NORTHERN ANDEAN COUNTRIES

THE ANDES MOUNTAINS extend down the whole length of South America, from north to south. They rise in Colombia, the country which borders the narrow land link with Central America, the Isthmus of Panama.

Colombia is a beautiful country with three ranges of the Andes running through it. The mountains slope east to grasslands and then to rainforest. The chief cities are on the coast, which is warm and humid, or in the cooler mountain regions. The mountains are mined for gold, emeralds, salt and coal.

The Andes rise to 6,267 metres above sea level at Chimborazo in **Ecuador**. Bananas and sugar-cane are grown here. In the cooler foothills of the Andes coffee is an important crop. To the east of the mountains are rainforests, where oil is drilled. Ecuador is the second largest oil producer in South America after Venezuela.

In the 1400s, **Peru** was the centre of the mighty Inca empire, an advanced Native American civilization which produced beautiful textiles and jewellery in gold and precious stones. Ruined Inca cities such as Machu Picchu still perch high amongst the peaks of the Andes. Terraced hillsides allow crops such as potatoes to be grown in the mountains. Fishing is important along the foggy Pacific coast. In the far east, rivers flow through tropical forests into the river Amazon.

Lake Titicaca lies high in the Andes on the border between Peru and **Bolivia**. Bolivia is an inland country which lies across the high plateau of the Altiplano, where most Bolivians live, and stretches into hot, humid rainforest in the east. The city of La Paz is the world's highest capital city, at 3,660 metres above sea level. Bolivia produces tin, timber, rubber and potatoes.

The lands of the northern Andes are home to many Native Americans, such as the Quechua and Aymara peoples. The whole region was ruled by Spain from the 1500s to the early 1800s, and Spanish is spoken throughout the region as well as a number of Native American languages. Although the region is rich in minerals and timber, many ordinary

N

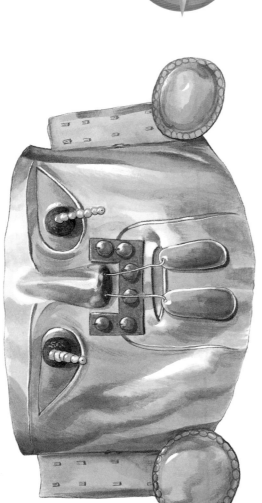

Inca crafts

This mask was made by Inca goldsmiths in Peru. The Incas came to power in the 1400s and were famous for their beautiful work with gold.

Point Gallinas

VENEZUELA

Barranquilla
Cartagena ● ▲ *Cristobal Colón*
5,775 m

Manizales
Medellín
Pereira ● ● Neiva
Ibagué ● ▲ *Nevado del Huila*
Cali ▽ 5,750 m

COLOMBIA
■ Bogotá

Meta
Guaviare

Magdalena
Cauca

Buenaventura

Cape Corrientes

Pasto ●

PANAMA

COLOMBIA

Point Galera

ECUADOR

Quito

Guayaquil ● ▲ *Chimborazo*
6,267 m
Gulf of Guayaquil

ECUADOR

Putumayo
Caquetá

Amazon

B R A Z I L

Iquitos ●

Marañón

●Piura

Point Aguja

PERU

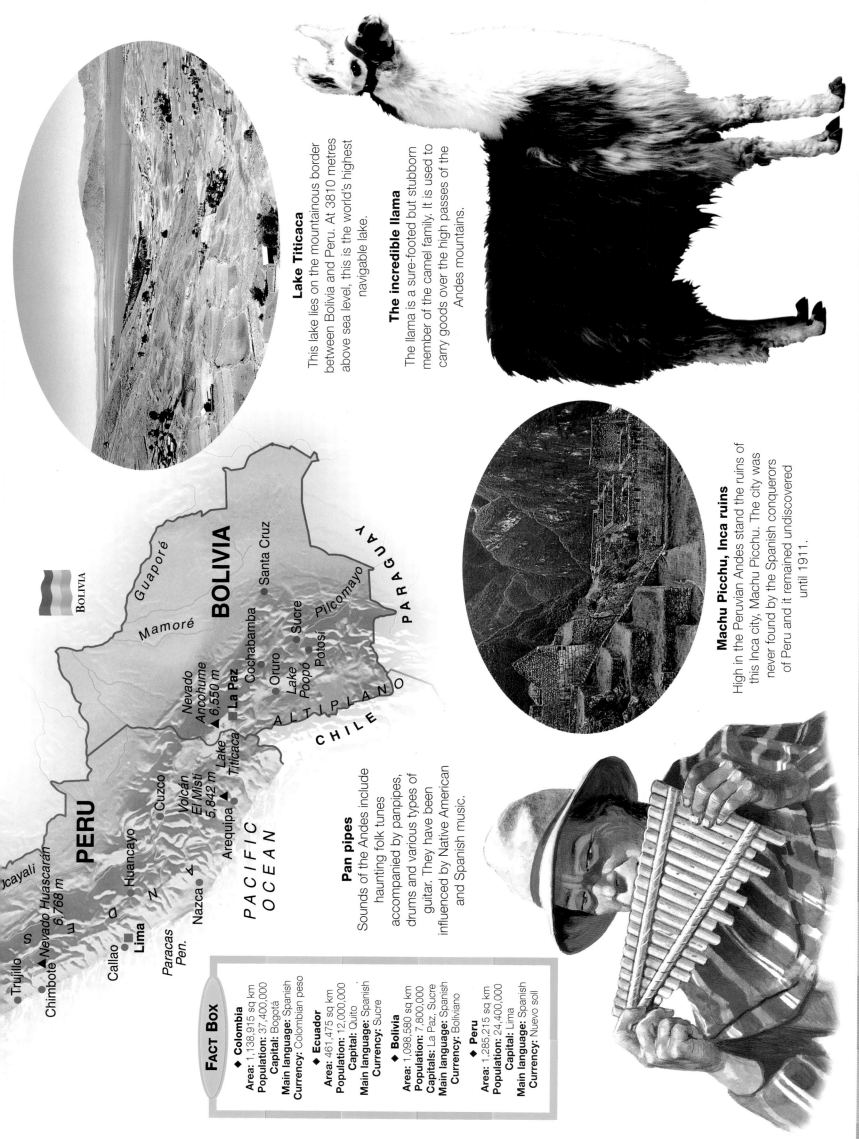

Lake Titicaca

This lake lies on the mountainous border between Bolivia and Peru. At 3810 metres above sea level, this is the world's highest navigable lake.

The incredible llama

The llama is a sure-footed but stubborn member of the camel family. It is used to carry goods over the high passes of the Andes mountains.

Machu Picchu, Inca ruins

High in the Peruvian Andes stand the ruins of this Inca city, Machu Picchu. The city was never found by the Spanish conquerors of Peru and it remained undiscovered until 1911.

Pan pipes

Sounds of the Andes include haunting folk tunes accompanied by panpipes, drums and various types of guitar. They have been influenced by Native American and Spanish music.

BOLIVIA

BOLIVIA

Guaporé

Mamoré

Santa Cruz

Cochabamba

Sucre

Pilcomayo

Oruro

Potosí

Lake
Poopó

Nevado
Ancohume
▲ 6,550 m

La Paz

ALTIPLANO

CHILE

PARAGUAY

PERU

Cuzco

Volcán
El Misti
▲ 5,842 m

Lake
Titicaca

Arequipa ●

Huancayo

Nazca ●

PACIFIC
OCEAN

Ucayali

Nevado Huascarán
▲ 6,768 m

Trujillo ●

Chimbote ●

Callao

Lima

Paracas
Pen.

FACT BOX

◆ **Colombia**
Area: 1,138,915 sq km
Population: 37,400,000
Capital: Bogotá
Main language: Spanish
Currency: Colombian peso

◆ **Ecuador**
Area: 461,475 sq km
Population: 12,000,000
Capital: Quito
Main language: Spanish
Currency: Sucre

◆ **Bolivia**
Area: 1,098,580 sq km
Population: 7,800,000
Capitals: La Paz, Sucre
Main language: Spanish
Currency: Boliviano

◆ **Peru**
Area: 1,285,215 sq km
Population: 24,400,000
Capital: Lima
Main language: Spanish
Currency: Nuevo soll

Gulf of
Venezuela
Netherlands
Antilles
Maracaibo
Caracas
Port of Spain
**TRINIDAD
& TOBAGO**
Lake
Maracaibo
ANDES MTS.
Barcelona
GUYANA
Pico Bolívar
5,002 m
LLANOS
Orinoco
Orinoco Delta
VENEZUELA
Angel
Falls
Georgetown
SURINAM
G U I A N A
Paramaribo
COLOMBIA
Orinoco
GUYANA
Cayenne
VENEZUELA
H I G H L A N D S
SURINAM
FRENCH GUIANA
Branco
Pico da Neblina
3014 m
Negro
Macapá
*Marajó
Bay*
**FRENCH
GUIANA**
Japurá
Amazon
Marajó I.
Belèm
*São
Marcos
Bay*
Manaus
Santarém
Tocantins
São Luis
S E L V A S
Madeira
Tapajós
Xingu
Teresina
Juruá
Purus
Aripuaná
Araguaia
Parnaiba
Rio Branco
Jiparaná
Arinos
BRAZIL
*Sobradinho
Reservoir*
PERU
*SERRA DOS PARECIS
Guaporé*
BOLIVIA
*MATO GROSSO
PLATEAU*
Coffee beans
Brazil is the world's biggest producer of
coffee. The crop is mostly grown in the south,
on large estates and is exported worldwide.
Cuiabá
Brasília
Goiânia
*BRAZILIAN
HIGHLANDS*
Uberlandia
Campo Grande
Belo Horizonte
Paraná
Campos
São Paulo
Rio de
Janeiro
*Cape
Frio*
Santos
PARAGUAY
Itaipu Res.
SERRA DO MAR
Curitiba
BRAZIL
Itguaçu
Falls
Florianópolis
ARGENTINA
Uruguay
N
Santa Maria
Pôrto Alegre
Patos Lagoon
URUGUAY
Mirim Lake

Rio panorama
A huge statue of Christ stands high above the
Brazilian port of Rio de Janeiro.

BRAZIL AND ITS NEIGHBOURS

BRAZIL is South America's largest nation. It includes grasslands, fertile plateaus and dry areas of scrub.

About a third of the country is taken up by tropical rainforests. All kinds of rare plants, parrots, snakes and monkeys live in these dense, dripping forests, which are under threat from road-builders, farmers, miners and loggers. The forests are crossed by hundreds of rivers, which drain into the wide, muddy waters of the Amazon, one of the world's two longest rivers. The river basin of the Amazon is the world's largest, covering 7,045,000 square kilometres.

Most Brazilians live in the big cities of the Atlantic coast, such as Rio de Janeiro and São Paolo. The country has rich resources, but many of the population are poor people who live in shacks built on the outskirts of the city. Brasília, with its broad avenues and high-rise buildings, was specially built as the country's new capital city in the 1960s.

To the northeast of Brazil, on the Caribbean coast, is **Venezuela**. This land, crossed by the Orinoco River, includes rainforests, high mountains and the tropical grassy plains of the Llanos. The beautiful Angel Falls (the world's highest at 979 metres) provide hydroelectric power, while Lake Maracaibo, in the northwest, is rich in oil.

The three other countries on the Caribbean coast are **Guyana**, **Surinam** and **French Guiana**. The first was once a British colony, the second was a Dutch colony and the third is still an overseas department governed by France. Most people live in the humid regions of the coast, while the rainforests and mountains of the remote south are more sparsely populated. Crops include sugar-cane, coffee, rice and bananas. An important mineral is bauxite, used in the making of aluminium.

Many different ethnic groups live in the region as a whole, including Native American peoples who have had to struggle to survive ever since Europeans invaded the region in the 1500s. The population of northern South America also includes many people of Asian, African, European and mixed descent, with ancestors from Spain, Portugal, Italy, Germany, France, Netherlands and Britain.

FACT BOX

◆ **Brazil**
Area: 8,511,965 sq km
Population: 160,300,000
Capital: Brasília
Main language: Portuguese
Currency: Cruzeiro real

◆ **Venezuela**
Area: 912,045 sq km
Population: 22,600,000
Capital: Caracas
Main language: Spanish
Currency: Bolívar

◆ **Guyana**
Area: 214,970 sq km
Population: 800,000
Capital: Georgetown
Main language: English
Currency: Guyana dollar

◆ **Surinam**
Area: 163,820 sq km
Population: 446,000
Capital: Paramaribo
Official language: Dutch
Currency: Surinam guilder

◆ **French Guiana**
Area: 91,000 sq km
Population: 300,000
Capital: Cayenne
Main language: French
Currency: French franc

Fortaleza
Natal
SERTÃO
Recife
São Francisco
Maceió
Salvador

Rainforest creatures
The vast forests which are drained by the River Amazon, support all kinds of wildlife, such as this brightly coloured macaw. Sadly, many species are threatened by the clearance of the forests by farmers and illegal traders in wildlife.

Fishing for a living
A fishing crew check their tackle as children play on the beach. This scene is near Salvador, capital of the tropical Bahía region in northeastern Brazil.

Yanomami hunters
About 13,000 Yanomami people live in Venezuela and another 8000 in Brazil. They live by hunting, fishing and growing food in the rainforest.

ARGENTINA AND ITS NEIGHBOURS

THE SOUTHERN PART of South America

stretches from the hot and humid Gran Chaco region to the cold and stormy waters of Tierra del Fuego and Cape Horn.

The largest country of this region is **Argentina**. Its highly populated capital is Buenos Aires on the river Plate. More than eight out of every ten Argentineans are city dwellers. However it was the country's cattle-farming regions – the Pampa grasslands and the northeast – that in the last 150 years brought wealth to the country and attracted large numbers of settlers from Europe. Argentina's western borders follow the high peak of the Andes range, which reach their highest point at Cerro Aconcagua (6,959 metres above sea level). To the south are the windswept plateaus of Patagonia, largely given over to sheep farming. The port of Ushuaia is the southernmost town in the world.

Northwards from Buenos Aires, across the river Plate, lies Montevideo, capital of **Uruguay**. This is another country which raises cattle and sheep, and whose rich grasslands and mild climate attracted European settlers. Neighbouring **Paraguay** is far from the coast. Most of its people farm the hills and plains of the east. Few live in the hot wilderness of the Gran Chaco.

To the west of the Andes is **Chile**, which covers a long and narrow area. Here is one of the driest regions on Earth, the Atacama desert. It also includes fertile orchards and productive vineyards, the big city of Santiago and the spectacular glaciers of the southern Andes. Spanish is spoken throughout the region, and some Native American languages such as Guaraní may also be heard.

Armadillo

The head and body of the armadillo is covered by an armour of plates made of horny and bony material. These usually nocturnal animals, feed mainly on insects and rest in a burrow by day.

Paraná River, Paraguay

Separating Paraguay and Argentina the Parana River flows some 4,500 km. The English explorer Sebastian Cabot was the first to sail up it in 1526.

BRAZIL

PARAGUAY
Concepción
Cuidad del Este
Asunción
Alto Paraná
Posadas
Paraguay
Corrientes
MESOPOTAMIA
Salto
Paysandú
Negro
URUGUAY
Montevideo
La Plata

G R A N   C H A C O
Verde
Pilcomayo
Bermejo
Formosa
Resistencia
Paraná
Concordia
Santa Fe
Paraná
Rosario
Buenos Aires
Salado
Mar Chiquito
Córdoba
Santiago del Estero
San Miguel de Tucumán
Catamarca
La Rioja
SIERRA DE CÓRDOBA
Río Cuarto
San Luis

BOLIVIA
Arica
Iquique
Antofagasta
Calama
Salta
S   A   N   D   E   S
Ojos del Salado 6,880 m ▲
Copiapó
San Juan
Mendoza
San Rafael
Aconcagua 6,959 m ▲
Valparaíso
Santiago
Rancagua
Coquimbo
Pta. Lengua de Vaca
ATACAMA DESERT
CHILE

PARAGUAY

40

Buenos Aires by night

The Monument of the Two Congresses stands in front of the domed Palace of Congress, built in 1906. The Argentinian capital is a large, lively city.

SOUTH GEORGIA (U.K.)

N

Prickly Pear

The flesh and seeds of the peeled fruit of the prickly pear have a pleasant taste. This cactus is low-growing and has flat oval stem joints and bright yellow flowers and occurs in Central and South America.

URUGUAY

ARGENTINA

P A M P A S

Salado

Talca

Chillán

Concepción
Pta. Lavapié

CHILE

Temuco

Valdivia
Pta. de la Galera
Osorno

Puerto Montt

Chiloé I.

C. Quilán

LOS CHONOS
ARCHIPELAGO

Wellington I.

REINA ADELAIDA
ARCHIPELAGO

Santa Inés I.

P A C I F I C
O C E A N

Neuquén
Negro
Limay

P A T A G O N I A

A N D E S

M

Lake Buenos
Aires

Chico

Chico

Deseado

Chubut

Colorado

Bahía Blanca

Bahía Blanca

Mar del Plata
Cape Corrientes

de La Plata
Pta. Norte
Cape San Antonio

Viedma

San Matías Gulf

Valdés Peninsula

Rawson

Comodoro Rivadavia
San Jorge Gulf
C. Tres Puntas
Puerto Deseado

Penas
Gulf

Santo Cruz

Puerto Santa Cruz

Bahía
Grande

Río Gallegos

Strait of Magellan

Punta Arenas

Tierra
del
Fuego

Ushuaia

C. San Diego

Cape Horn

ARGENTINA

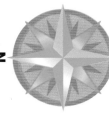

FALKLAND/MALVINAS
ISLANDS

West
Falkland

Stanley
East
Falkland

Mountains, Southern Chile

The long, narrow country of Chile has vast differences in climate. There is hot desert in the north, Mediterranean type in the centre and cool, humid conditions in the south. Some mountains are permanently snow-capped.

41

Turkish women

These women are from the port of Kas in southern Turkey. They are kneading dough and making pastry. Many Muslim women cover their heads with scarves or full veils.

ASIA

SOUTHWEST ASIA

SOUTHWEST ASIA IS SOMETIMES described as the Near East or the Middle East. Its peoples include Greek Cypriots, Turks, Jews, Arabs, Kurds and Iranians.

The region has seen many political disputes and wars in recent years – between Greeks and Turks on Cyprus, between Palestinian Arabs and Jews in Israel, between Iraqi and Iranians and between Iraqui and Kuwaiti Arabs. The Kurds, whose homeland is occupied by **Iraq**, **Iran** and **Turkey**, have also been at the centre of conflict.

It was in Southwest Asia that the world's first civilizations grew up, between the rivers Tigris and Euphrates, over 6,000 years ago. The region later gave birth to three world faiths – Judaism, Christianity and Islam. In the days of the Roman empire the Jews were scattered from their homeland, and over the centuries their culture spread to Spain, Central and Eastern Europe and the Americas. Arab armies and traders took the Islamic faith into Africa and Spain, and Arab scholars made great advances in mathematics and astronomy. From the 1500s the Turks established a great empire which stretched from Central Europe to the Indian Ocean.

Southwest Asia includes vast deserts, in the Arabian peninsula and in eastern Iran. It also takes in fertile plains, the marshes of southern Iraq and mountain ranges of Turkey and Iran. The north of the region borders the Black Sea and the Caspian Sea, grassy steppes and the Caucasus mountains. To the east lies Afghanistan, Pakistan and the Indian sub-continent.

The region's most valuable resource is oil, which brings wealth to the governments of the lands around the Persian Gulf. However many ordinary people of Southwest Asia remain poor, living by herding goats, sheep or camels. In Israel and some other regions irrigation has made it possible to grow crops in harsh, dry environments. Oranges, dates, grapes and many kinds of nuts are grown in the region.

A summons to prayer

Mosques, like this one in Kuwait, have tall towers called minarets. From here, faithful Muslims are called to prayer. This message is often broadcast from loudspeakers. Muslims are expected to pray five times a day.

Map labels

Istanbul · **TURKEY** · **SYRIA** · Samsun · **BLACK SEA** · Gallipoli · *Sakarya* · **PONTIC MOUNTAINS** · Bursa · Eskisehir · **Ankara** · *Tuz Lake* · *Kizil* · Izmir · **T U R K E Y** · Kayseri · *Lake Van* · Konya · Gaziantep · Diyarbakir · Antalya · **TAURUS MTS.** · Adana · Aleppo · Mosul · *Tigris* · **CYPRUS** · *Euphrates* · **Nicosia** · **S Y R I A** · **CYPRUS** · Limassol · Tripoli · Homs · **SYRIAN DESERT** · **LEBANON** · **I R A Q** · **LEBANON** · **Beirut** · **Damascus** · Haifa · Karbala · **ISRAEL** · Tel Aviv · **Amman** · **Jerusalem** · **ISRAEL** · **JORDAN** · **EGYPT** · Elat · Al Jawf · Sakakah · **A N   N A F U D** · Buraydah · **JORDAN** · Medina · **S A U D I** · *HIJAZ* · *RED SEA* · Jiddah · Mecca · *ASIR* · *Tihamah* · *Jabal Sawda 3,133 m* · *Jaza'ir Farasan* · **SAUDI ARABIA** · Al Hudaydah · *Bab al Mandab*

Wealth from oil
These supertankers are taking oil on board, off the coast of Saudi Arabia. Wealth from oil has transformed the economy of the Middle East and given great power to the many small countries around the Persian Gulf.

IRAQ

Mt. Ararat
5,185 m

Aras

CASPIAN SEA

Tabriz

Lake Urmia

Rasht

ELBURZ MTS.

Babol

▲ Mt. Damavand
5,604 m

As Sulaymaniyah

Kirkuk

Hamadan

Tehran

Qom

Mashhad

TURKMENISTAN

N

KUWAIT

Bakhtaran

ZAGROS MOUNTAINS

Baghdad

Kashan

Dasht-e-Kavir

I R A N

Esfahan

AFGHANISTAN

Dasht-e-Lut

BAHRAIN

An Nasiriyah

Ahvaz

Yazd

Basra

Abadan

Kerman

IRAN

KUWAIT

Kuwait

Shiraz

Zahedan

Bushehr

The Gulf

Bandar Abbas

Ad Dahna

Ad Damman

Bandar e Lengeh

Jask

Strait of Hormuz

Al Manamah

Gulf of Oman

Shaqra

BAHRAIN

QATAR

Doha

Dubai

Abu Dhabi

Riyadh

UNITED ARAB EMIRATES

QATAR

Muscat

▲ Jabal Ash Sham
3,035 m

A R A B I A

Sur

UNITED ARAB EMIRATES

O M A N

Masirah I.

OMAN

Rub' al Khali
(Empty Quarter)

On the move
In many parts of Southwest Asia people live as nomads, wandering with their herds from one pasture to another, or following ancient trade routes.

Salalah

Kuria Muria Is.

Tarim

Hadramaut

San'a

YEMEN

YEMEN

Al Mukalla

Gulf of Aden

Socotra (YEMEN)

'Abd al kuri

Aden

INDIA AND ITS NEIGHBOURS

SOUTHERN ASIA stretches south into the Indian Ocean, forming a landmass so large that it sometimes called the 'sub-continent'. Its northern limits are marked by the Himalaya and Karakoram mountain ranges. These include many of the world's highest peaks and reach 8,848 metres above sea level at Everest, on Nepal's border with China.

The ranges pass through eastern Afghanistan, the Kashmir region on the border of India and Pakistan, India itself and the small mountain kingdoms of **Nepal** and **Bhutan**. Melting snows flow south from the mountains to form the five great rivers of the Punjab and also the mighty Ganges, which winds across the fertile plains of northern India before crossing Bangladesh into a maze of waterways around the Bay of Bengal. This area suffers from devastating floods.

Central and southern **India** form a triangular plateau called the Deccan, fringed on the east and west by the mountainous Ghats. These slopes are forested, catching the full force of the monsoon winds which bring rains from the Indian Ocean. For most of the year India is extremely hot and dry. Indian Ocean nations include the beautiful, tropical island of **Sri Lanka** and a chain of very low coral islands, the **Maldives.**

Advanced civilizations had developed around the river Indus by about 2500BC, and great religions grew up in India over the ages, including Hinduism, Buddhism and Sikhism. Invaders and traders brought Islam to the region. India today is a fascinating mixture of cultures, with over 800 different languages and dialects. There are many different customs, dress and foods. Spicy dishes from India are now popular everywhere.

The Indian sub-continent has a vast population, with many hungry mouths to feed. Many people make their living by farming, growing wheat, rice, millet, sugar-cane, coconut and tea. Most industries are based in the highly populated cities of India and Pakistan.

Himalayan peaks

Breathtaking Mount Makalu, on the border between Nepal and China, rises to 8,470 metres above sea level. Eighty-eight percent of the world's mountains over 7,315 metres rise within the Himalaya-Karakoram ranges, many of them in the kingdom of Nepal.

AFGHANISTAN

PAKISTAN

TURKMENISTAN

TAJIKISTAN

Mazar-e-Sharif

Herat

Farah

AFGHANISTAN

HINDU

Kabul

Khyber Pass

Peshawar

Qandahar

Quetta

RIGESTAN DESERT

BALUCHISTAN PLATEAU

PAKISTAN

SULAIMAN RANGE

Karachi

Gulf of Kachch

Hyderabad

Sukkur

Indus

Bahawalpur

Multan

Sutlej

Faisalabad Lahore

Rawalpindi

Islamabad

Srinagar

JAMMU & KASHMIR

DISPUTED AREA

KARAKORAM

K2 8,611m

PUNJAB

Amritsar

GREAT INDIAN DESERT (THAR DESERT)

Jodhpur

Ajmer

Jaipur

Udaipur

Kota

Gwalior

Delhi

New Delhi

Agra

Yamuna

Bareilly

Lucknow

Kanpur

Allahabad

Varanasi

Nanda Devi 7,817m

Annapurna 8,078m

NEPAL

Katmandu

Ghagara

Ganges

Patna

Tibet (CHINA)

Mt Everest 8,848m

Thimphu

BHUTAN

NEPAL

BHUTAN

Brahmaputra

Gauhati

NAGA HILLS

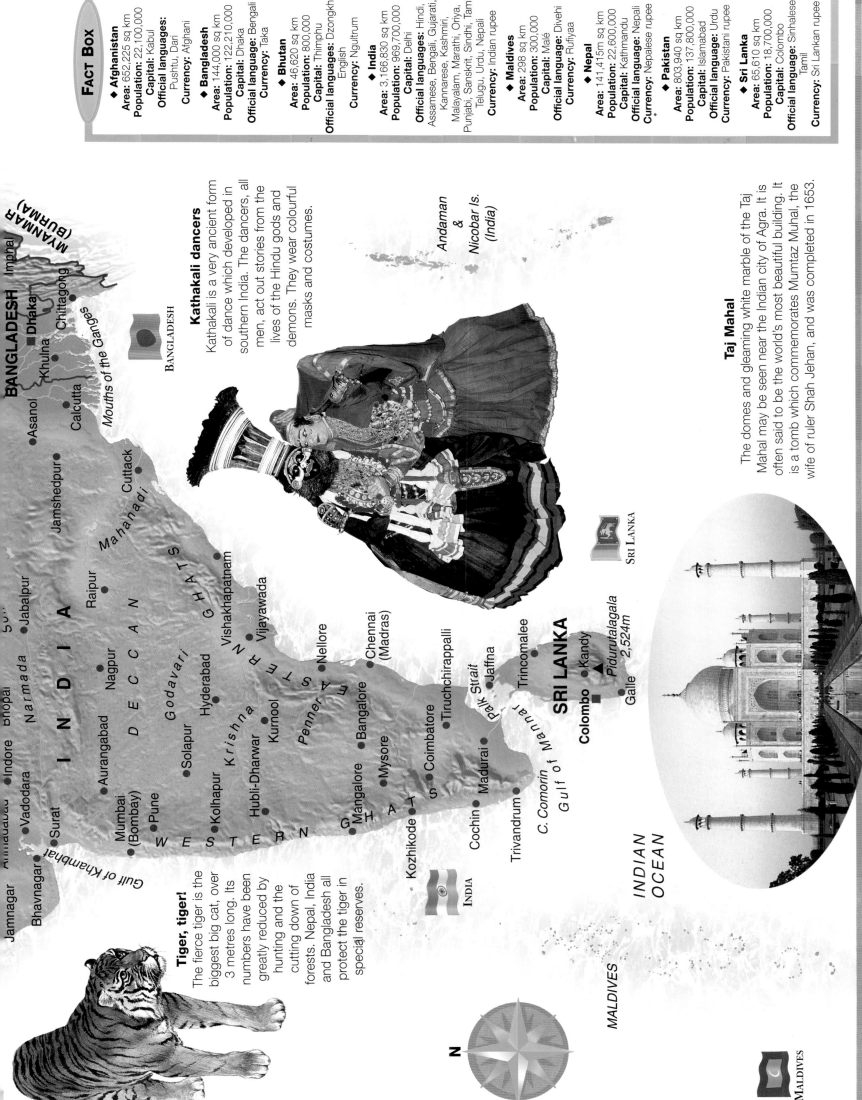

◆ **Afghanistan**
Area: 652,225 sq km
Population: 22,100,000
Capital: Kabul
Official languages:
Pushtu, Dari
Currency: Afghani

◆ **Bangladesh**
Area: 144,000 sq km
Population: 122,210,000
Capital: Dhaka
Official language: Bengali
Currency: Taka

◆ **Bhutan**
Area: 46,620 sq km
Population: 800,000
Capital: Thimphu
Official languages: Dzongkha,
English
Currency: Ngultrum

◆ **India**
Area: 3,166,830 sq km
Population: 969,700,000
Capital: Delhi
Official languages: Hindi,
Assamese, Bengali, Gujarati,
Kannarese, Kashmiri,
Malayalam, Marathi, Oriya,
Punjabi, Sanskrit, Sindhi, Tamil,
Telugu, Urdu, Nepali
Currency: Indian rupee

◆ **Maldives**
Area: 298 sq km
Population: 300,000
Capital: Malé
Official language: Divehi
Currency: Rufiyaa

◆ **Nepal**
Area: 141,415m sq km
Population: 22,600,000
Capital: Kathmandu
Official language: Nepali
Currency: Nepalese rupee

◆ **Pakistan**
Area: 803,940 sq km
Population: 137,800,000
Capital: Islamabad
Official language: Urdu
Currency: Pakistani rupee

◆ **Sri Lanka**
Area: 65,610 sq km
Population: 18,700,000
Capital: Colombo
Official language: Sinhalese,
Tamil
Currency: Sri Lankan rupee

Kathakali dancers

Kathakali is a very ancient form of dance which developed in southern India. The dancers, all men, act out stories from the lives of the Hindu gods and demons. They wear colourful masks and costumes.

Taj Mahal

The domes and gleaming white marble of the Taj Mahal may be seen near the Indian city of Agra. It is often said to be the world's most beautiful building. It is a tomb which commemorates Mumtaz Muhal, the wife of ruler Shah Jehan, and was completed in 1653.

Tiger, tiger!

The fierce tiger is the biggest big cat, over 3 metres long. Its numbers have been greatly reduced by hunting and the cutting down of forests. Nepal, India and Bangladesh all protect the tiger in special reserves.

45

CHINA AND ITS NEIGHBOURS

CHINA is the world's third largest country in area, and has a higher population than any other. It is bordered by the world's highest mountains, by deserts and by tropical seas.

Most people live in the big industrial cities of the south and east and on the fertile plains around two great rivers, the Huang He and the Chiang Jiang. Crops include wheat, maize, tea, sugar-cane and rice. Rice is eaten with almost every meal.

Chinese civilization dates back over thousands of years. Chinese inventions included paper and gunpowder and Chinese crafts included the making of fine porcelain and silk. Since 1949 China has been ruled by its Communist Party, but its politics are no longer really socialist. Its economy has become one of the most important in the Pacific region, and in 1997 it took back the territory of Hong Kong, an international centre of business which had been a British colony. China also claims the island of **Taiwan**, which is still governed independently by Chinese nationalists who lost power in 1949.

The **Korean peninsula** saw bitter fighting between 1950 and 1953, when Korea divided into two nations, North and South. These countries remain bitter enemies today. South Korea has become an important industrial power.

Far to the north the Mongol peoples live in the independent republic of **Mongolia**. This includes the barren Gobi desert and remote grasslands.

KAZAKHSTAN

Ulaangom

Fuhai · Hovd

ALTAI MTS.

HANGAYI

Ebinur Hu · Karamay

Yining · Kuytun · Dzungaria

KYRGYZSTAN

TIAN SHAN

Ürümqi · Hami

Bosten Lake · Turfan Depression

Aksu

Kashi

TAKLIMAKAN DESERT

Yumen

ALTUN SHAN

Hotan

▲ Mt. K2

KARAKORAM

KUNLUN SHAN

INDIA

HI

M

PLATEAU OF TIBET

Siling Lake · TANGGULA SHAN

Tangra Lake

Nam Lake

Lhasa

Mt. Everest ▲ 8,848 m

Xigaze

NEPAL

L

A

Y

A

BHUTAN

Temple of Heaven
Tiantan, the Temple of Heaven in Beijing, is a beautiful group of buildings first raised in 1420. The Chinese emperors used to come here to pray for a good harvest.

The Great Wall
A defensive wall runs across the north of China for about 6,000 kilometres, with many extra twists and turns. It was started in about 246 BC and added to over hundreds of years.

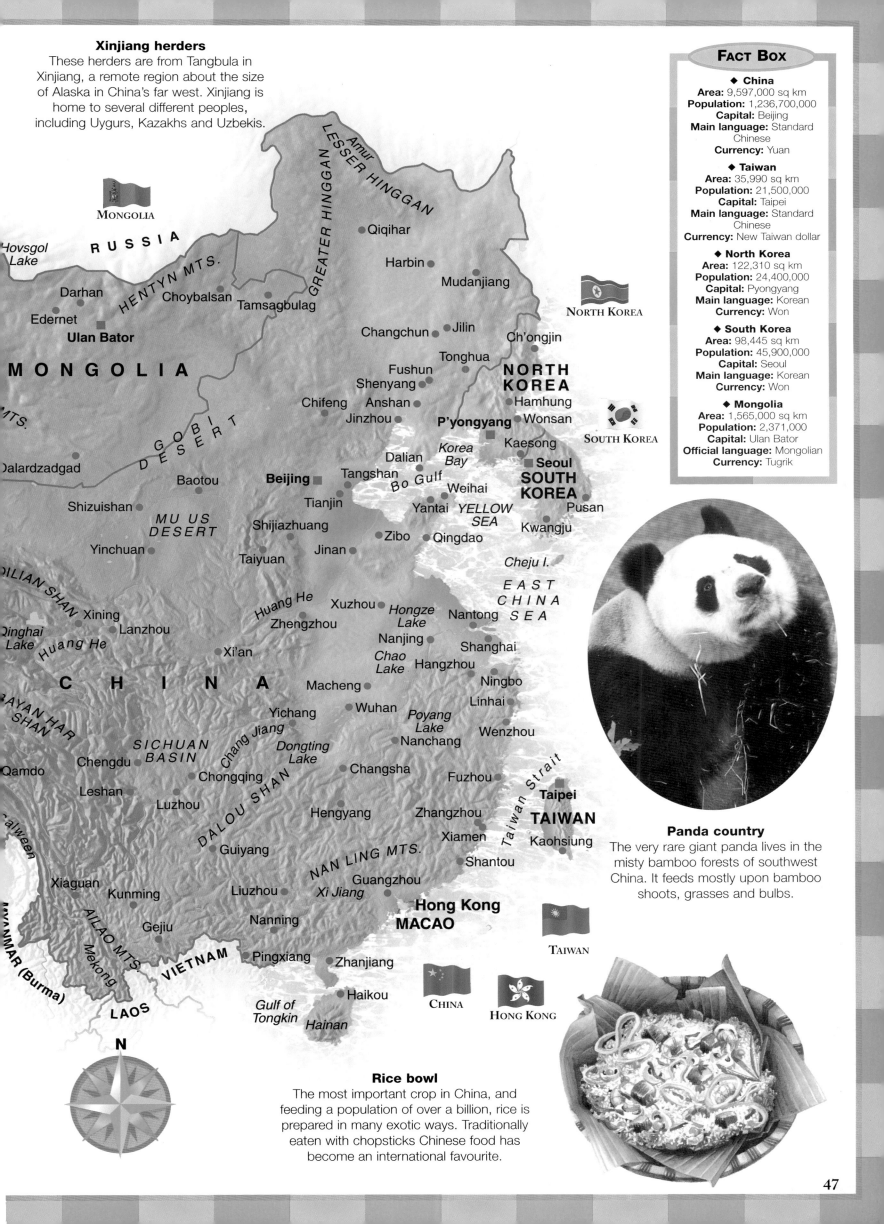

Xinjiang herders
These herders are from Tangbula in Xinjiang, a remote region about the size of Alaska in China's far west. Xinjiang is home to several different peoples, including Uygurs, Kazakhs and Uzbekis.

MONGOLIA

RUSSIA

Hovsgol Lake

Amur

GREATER HINGGAN

LESSER HINGGAN

Darhan
Edernet
Choybalsan
Tamsagbulag
HENTYN MTS.

Qiqihar

Harbin
Mudanjiang

Ulan Bator

MONGOLIA

Changchun
Jilin
Ch'ongjin

Tonghua

NORTH KOREA

Fushun
Shenyang
Chifeng
Anshan
Jinzhou

Hamhung

P'yongyang
Wonsan

G O B I   D E S E R T

Dalardzadgad

Baotou

Beijing
Tangshan

Dalian

Korea Bay

Kaesong

Seoul

SOUTH KOREA

SOUTH KOREA

Shizuishan

MU US DESERT

Tianjin

Bo Gulf

Weihai

Yinchuan

Shijiazhuang

Jinan

Zibo
Qingdao

Yantai
YELLOW SEA

Pusan
Kwangju

Taiyuan

Cheju I.

DILIAN SHAN

Xining
Lanzhou

Qinghai Lake

Huang He

Huang He
Xuzhou
Zhengzhou

Hongze Lake

Nantong

E A S T   C H I N A   S E A

Nanjing

Shanghai

Xi'an

Chao Lake
Hangzhou

CHINA

Macheng

Ningbo
Linhai

AYAN HAR SHAN

Yichang

Wuhan

Poyang Lake

Wenzhou

SICHUAN BASIN

Chang Jiang

Dongting Lake

Nanchang

Qamdo

Chengdu

Chongqing

Changsha

Fuzhou

Leshan

Luzhou

DALOU SHAN

Hengyang

Zhangzhou

Xiamen

Taiwan Strait

Taipei

TAIWAN

Xiaguan

Guiyang

NAN LING MTS.

Kaohsiung

Kunming

Liuzhou

Guangzhou

Shantou

AILAO MTS.

Gejiu

Nanning

Xi Jiang

Hong Kong
MACAO

Salween

Mekong

VIETNAM

Pingxiang

Zhanjiang

MYANMAR (Burma)

LAOS

Haikou

Gulf of Tongkin

Hainan

CHINA

HONG KONG

N

NORTH KOREA

SOUTH KOREA

TAIWAN

Panda country
The very rare giant panda lives in the misty bamboo forests of southwest China. It feeds mostly upon bamboo shoots, grasses and bulbs.

Rice bowl
The most important crop in China, and feeding a population of over a billion, rice is prepared in many exotic ways. Traditionally eaten with chopsticks Chinese food has become an international favourite.

JAPAN

JAPAN is made up of over 3,000 islands, and these stretch for about 3,000 kilometres from north to south on the northwest rim of the Pacific Ocean.

The chief islands are called Hokkaido, Honshu, Shikoku and Kyushu. The islands extend from the tropical south to the chilly north, where winter snowfalls can be heavy. The region is a danger zone for earthquakes and Japan's highest mountain, Fuji, is a volcano.

The snow-covered slopes of Mount Fuji have been a favourite subject for Japanese artists over the years. Japan has a long history of excellence in art, theatre, poetry, architecture and pottery. Japanese civilization dates back over 2,000 years. The country has been ruled by emperors and, during the Middle Ages, it was fought over by powerful warlords and bands of knights called samurai. Faiths include Buddhism and Shinto, the country's traditional religion.

Japan is very mountainous and so land that is suitable for farming is very precious. Japanese farmers grow rice, tea and fruit and the country also has a large fishing fleet. Many meals are based on rice or fish. Japan has very few natural resources. Even so, over the last 50 years Japan has become a leading world producer of cars, televisions and other electrical goods.

The mountains also limit the spread of housing and so Japan's cities are mostly crowded on to the strip of flat land around the coast. Tokyo has spread out to join up with neighbouring cities, and now has a population of over 25 million.

The Japanese people make up 99 percent of the country's population. The remainder includes Koreans and the Ainu of the far north, who may be descended from the first people to inhabit Japan.

Mount Fuji

The beautiful peak of Mount Fuji, to the southwest of Tokyo, is a national symbol and, traditionally, a sacred mountain.

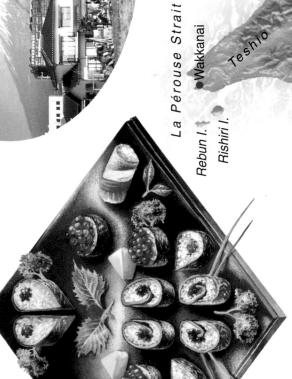

Sushi

Prawns, raw fish, seaweed, pickles and vegetables are used to make these tasty snacks. Like most Japanese dishes, they are served with rice. Japanese food is often beautifully arranged and thoughtfully served.

Tea time

Tea is harvested on the inland slopes. The Japanese are great tea-drinkers and have an ancient ceremony at which tea is specially prepared and served.

FACT BOX

◆ **Japan**
Area: 369,700 sq km
Population: 126,100,000
Capital: Tokyo
Main language: Japanese
Currency: Yen

Kuril Is. (Russia)

JAPAN

La Pérouse Strait

Rebun I.
Rishiri I.

● Wakkanai

Teshio

H o k k a i d o

● Asahigawa

▲ Asahi Mt.
2,290 m

● Kushiro

● Obihiro

Erimo Cape

Ishikari

Ishikari Bay

● Otaru
● Sapporo

● Muroran

Uchiura Bay

● Hakodate

Tsugaru Strait

Mutsa Bay

● Aomori
● Hirosaki

● Hachinohe

● Kamaishi

● Morioka

Kitakami

● Akita

*S E A
O F
J A P A N*

Sumo wrestlers

The ancient sport of sumo is still very popular in Japan. Super heavyweight wrestlers aim to ground their opponents or force them out of the ring. There are long ceremonies before each contest.

Itsukushima, Japan

Japan has many ancient Shinto shrines and Buddhist temples and many of these are set in beautiful scenery or gardens. Japan has always produced very simple and beautiful architecture and design.

A Shinto wedding

Dressed in her beautiful silk robe, or kimono, a Japanese bride sits next to her new husband, who also wears traditional costume. The wedding has been a Shinto ceremony. Shinto is an ancient Japanese faith which honours ancestors and the spirits of nature.

Ride the Bullet

Japan's Bullet Train offers one of the world's most famous passenger express services. It speeds across the country, linking the capital, Tokyo, with other large cities.

N

JAPAN

Sakata
Sendai
Yamagata
Iwaki
Abukuma
Hitachi
Niigata
Fukushima
Koriyama
Mito
Sado
Nagaoka
Utsunomiya
Chiba
Shinano
Ueda
Takasaki
Tokyo
Matsumoto
Yokohama
JAPANESE ALPS
Kofu
Kawasaki
Sagami Bay
Toyama
Mt. Fuji 3,776 m
O-shima
Kanazawa
Gifu
Shizuoka
Miyake I.
Fukui
Takefu
Toyota
Hamamatsu
Nagoya
Matsusaka
Biwa Lake
Kyoto
Sakai
Wakayama
Kobe
Osaka
Hachijo I.

Oki Is.

Honshu

Matsue
Okayama
Takamatsu
Inland Sea
Tokushima
Kii Channel
Hiroshima
Shikoku
Suo Sea
Matsuyama
Kochi
Bungo Channel

Tsushima
Kitakyushu
Fukuoka
Kyushu
Sasebo
Omuta
Kumamoto
Miyazaki
Nagasaki
Amakusa Is.
Sendai
Koshiki Is.
Kagoshima
Tanega
Yaku

PACIFIC OCEAN

49

SOUTHEAST ASIA

MYANMAR is a beautiful land lying between the hill country of India and China. It is crossed by the great Irrawaddy river, which flows south into the Indian Ocean. To the southeast is **Thailand**, a country green with rice fields and teak forests. To the west lie the lands once known as Indo-China – **Laos**, **Cambodia** and, on the long Mekong River, **Vietnam**.

Linked to the Asian mainland by a narrow isthmus, or strip of land, is **Malaysia**. This country also takes up the northern part of the island of **Borneo**, which it shares with the small oil-rich state of **Brunei**. Malaysia produces rubber, rice, tea and palm oil. Kuala Lumpur is a growing centre of international business with the 452 metre-high Petronas Towers, the world's highest building. **Singapore**, a small independent city state built on the islands across the Johor Strait, is another leader in the business world.

Indonesia makes up the world's largest island chain. It covers over 13,600 islands, which include Sumatra, Java, southern Borneo, Bali and Irian Jaya (the western half of New Guinea). Another large island chain, the **Philippines**, lie between the Pacific and the South China Sea.

All the islands bordering the Pacific Ocean lie in a danger zone for earthquakes and volcanoes. The region as a whole has a warm, often humid, climate, with monsoon winds bringing heavy rains. Southeast Asia's dwindling tropical forests are a last reserve for the region's rich wildlife, such as enormous butterflies and giant apes called orang-utans.

Many different peoples live in Southeast Asia, including Burmese, Thais, Vietnamese and Filippinos. There are also many people of Chinese and Indian descent. Buddhism is a major faith in the region. Most Indonesians are Muslims and the Philippines are largely Roman Catholic. During the last 50 years Southeast Asia has been torn apart by wars. The region now looks forward to a period of peace.

The face of a demon
This fierce-looking demon guards the gate of the Grand Palace in Bangkok, the capital of Thailand. Many tourists come to this kingdom, once known as Siam, to see its ancient temples and enjoy its beautiful scenery and beaches.

A dome of gold
The fantastic roofs of Shwe Dagon pagoda shimmer with gold. This holy site is in Yangon, capital city of Myanmar or Burma. The pagoda honours Gautama Buddha, the founder of the Buddhist faith.

Javanese carving
These beautiful figures, carved from stone, decorate Barobodur, on the island of Java. This 9th-century temple is the most splendid in Indonesia. Its carvings show scenes from the life of the Buddha.

PHILIPPINES

Laoag
Luzon
Mt. Pinatubo ▲
■ **Manila**
Mindoro

PHILIPPINES

Panay
Iloilo
Palawan
Negros
Tacloban
Cebu City
Bohol

SULU SEA

Mindanao

Zamboanga
Davao
Mt. Apo 2,954 m

INDONESIA

Bandar Seri Begawan
Mt. Kinabalu 4,094 m ▲
Sandakan
SABAH

BRUNEI
SARAWAK
Kapuas
BORNEO
Balikpapan
Palu

CELEBES SEA

Manado

MOLUCCA SEA

Halmahera

Moluccas
Sorong
Jayapura

IRIAN JAYA

NEW GUINEA

Barito
Banjarmasin
Ujung Pandang
Sulawesi

CERAM SEA
Seram
Buru
Ambon

I N D O N E S I A

BANDA SEA

Puncak Jaya
5,030m ▲

Aru Is.

Digul

PAPUA NEW GUINEA

SEA
Surabaya
Bali
Malang
Lombok
FLORES SEA
Sumbawa
Flores
Ende
Baubau
Wetar
Timor
Sumba
Kupang

Tanimbar Islands

Floating market
At a Thai market, fruit, vegetables or fish may be sold from small boats. These women traders wear broad-brimmed straw hats to protect them from the tropical sun and the heavy monsoon rains.

N

Kuala Lumpur
High-rise buildings are influenced by traditional styles in Kuala Lumpur, capital of Malaysia. 'KL' is one of the most important centres of industry, and business in Southeast Asia.

Komodo dragon
Meet the biggest lizard in the world, 3 metres long and weighing in at up to 136 kilograms. It is found on four small islands in Indonesia, called Rintja, Flores, Padar and Komodo.

AFRICA

NORTH AND WEST AFRICA

THE **SAHARA** IS THE WORLD'S LARGEST DESERT, made up of over 9 million square kilometres of baking hot sand, gravel and rock.

Its northern fringes, occupied by **Morocco**, **Algeria**, **Tunisia** and **Libya**, run into the milder, more fertile lands of the Mediterranean coast and the Atlas mountain ranges. They are home to Arabs and Berbers.

Deserts stretch from the Sahara eastwards to **Egypt** and the Red Sea. In ancient times one of the greatest civilizations the world has seen grew up in Egypt. Then as now, the country depended on water from the world's longest

Water for sale
A Berber water seller walks the streets of Marrakech, in Morocco, offering metal cups to passers-by.

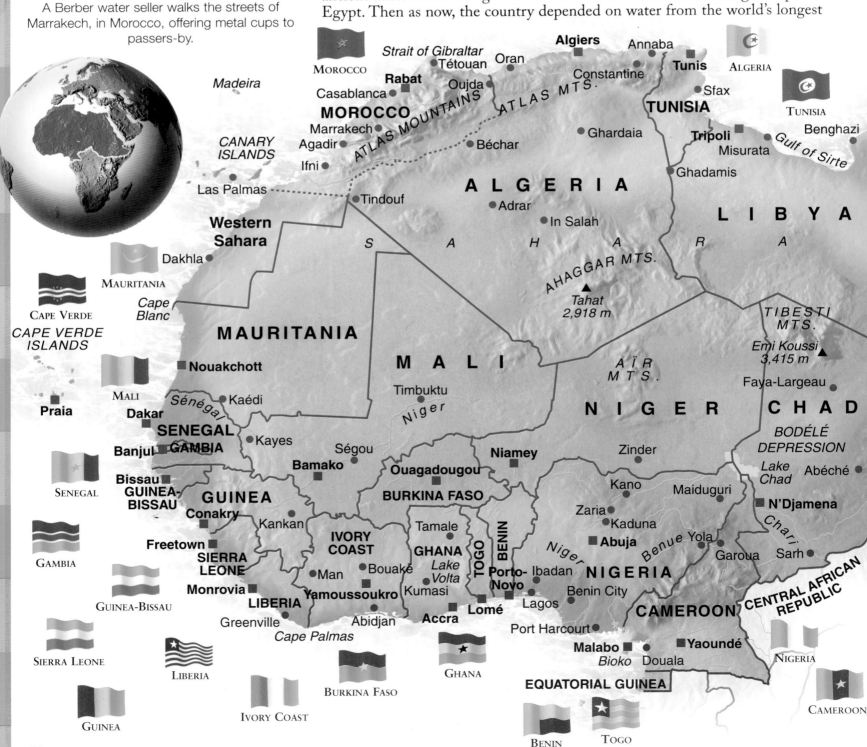

52

river, the Nile. This flows north to the Mediterranean from the mountains of **Ethiopia** and the swamps of southern **Sudan**, Africa's largest country.

The region south of the Sahara is known as the Sahel. It includes **Senegal**, **Mauritania**, **Mali**, **Niger**, **Burkina Faso** and **Chad**. The people include the Fulani, Kanuri and Hausa. The thin grasslands of the Sahel allow cattle herding, but droughts are common and the desert is spreading. Many people are very poor.

Thirteen nations border the great bulge of the West African coast, around the Gulf of Guinea. The coastal strip is made up of lagoons and long sandy beaches fringed with palm trees. Inland there is a belt of forest, which rises to dry, sandy plateaus and semi-desert in the far north. West African history tells of African kingdoms and empires which grew up here long ago, but also of the cruel slave trade across the Atlantic, which lasted from the 1500s to the 1800s. In the 1800s, large areas of West Africa became colonies of Britain and France. Today these lands are independent. The region has rich resources, including oil and diamonds.

Abu Simbel
When the new Aswan dam was being built in the 1960s this great temple of the ancient Egyptian ruler Rameses II had to be moved stone-by-stone.

N

CENTRAL, EASTERN & SOUTHERN AFRICA

CENTRAL AFRICA is dominated by the river Congo, which flows through hot and humid rainforest to the Atlantic Ocean. The great river winds through the **Democratic Republic of the Congo**, and the network of waterways which drain into it provide useful transport routes for riverboats and canoes.

A long crack in the Earth's crust, the Great Rift Valley, runs all the way down **East Africa**. Its route is marked by volcanoes and lakes. Some East African mountains remain snow-capped all year round, even though they are on the Equator. The highest of these is Kilimanjaro, at 5,950 metres. It looks out over savanna, grasslands dotted with trees. Huge herds of wildlife roam these plains. Zebra, giraffe, elephants and lions are protected within national parks. The Indian Ocean coast includes white beaches and coral islands. Mombasa, Dar-es-Salaam and Maputo are major ports.

In southern Africa the Drakensberg mountains descend to grassland known as veld. There are harsh deserts too, the Kalahari and the Namib. The **Republic of South Africa** is one of the most powerful countries in Africa. It has ports at Durban and Capetown.

Central and southern Africa are rich in mineral resources, including gold, diamonds and copper. Eastern and southern Africa are important farming regions, raising cattle and producing coffee, vegetables, tropical fruits, tobacco, and grape vines.

African kingdoms flourished in the Congo region in the Middle Ages and the stone ruins of Great Zimbabwe recall gold traders of long ago. Today the region is home to hundreds of African peoples with many different languages and cultures.

Magnificent Masai
This young Masai girl wears her traditional beaded necklace and headdress. These noble, nomadic people herd cattle and live mainly in Kenya and Tanzania.

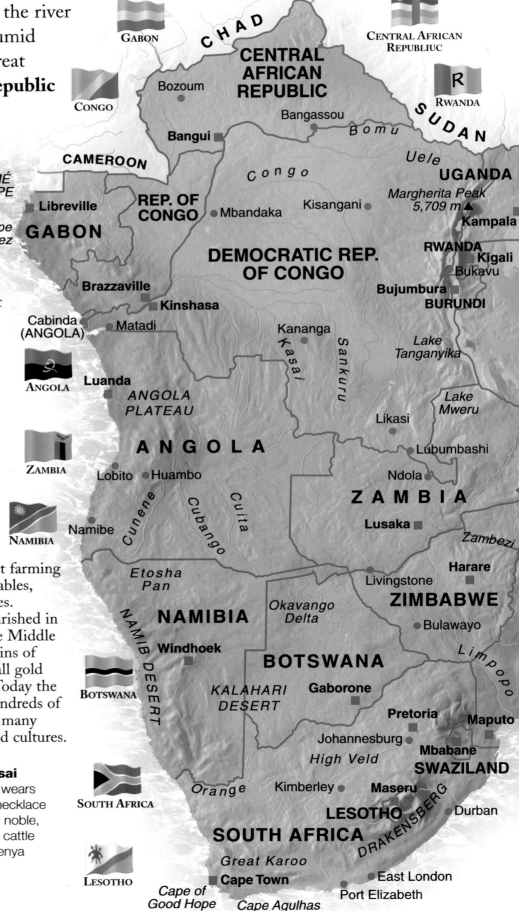

GABON

CHAD

CENTRAL AFRICAN REPUBLIUC

RWANDA

CONGO

CENTRAL AFRICAN REPUBLIC

Bozoum

Bangassou

Bangui

Bomu

SUDAN

CAMEROON

Congo

Uele

UGANDA

SÃO TOMÉ & PRÍNCIPE

REP. OF CONGO

Kisangani

Margherita Peak 5,709 m ▲

Libreville

Mbandaka

Kampala

Cape Lopez

GABON

RWANDA

Kigali

Bukavu

Brazzaville

DEMOCRATIC REP. OF CONGO

Bujumbura

Kinshasa

Cabinda (ANGOLA)

Matadi

Kananga

BURUNDI

Kasai

Sankuru

Lake Tanganyika

ANGOLA

Luanda

ANGOLA PLATEAU

Lake Mweru

Likasi

Lubumbashi

A N G O L A

Lobito · Huambo

ZAMBIA

Ndola

Z A M B I A

Namibe

Cunene

Cubango

Cuita

Lusaka

Zambezi

NAMIBIA

Etosha Pan

Okavango Delta

Livingstone

Harare

ZIMBABWE

NAMIBIA

Windhoek

BOTSWANA

Bulawayo

Limpopo

BOTSWANA

KALAHARI DESERT

Gaborone

NAMIB DESERT

Pretoria

Maputo

Johannesburg

Mbabane

SOUTH AFRICA

High Veld

SWAZILAND

Orange

Kimberley

Maseru

LESOTHO

Durban

SOUTH AFRICA

DRAKENSBERG

LESOTHO

Great Karoo

Cape Town

East London

Cape of Good Hope

Cape Agulhas

Port Elizabeth

La Digue, Seychelles
Over 100 islands make up the Seychelles. La Digue is only 15 square kilometres in area, but the third most populated.

Cape Caseyr

Berbera

SOMALIA

KENYA

UGANDA

E T H I O P I A

N

Lake Turkana

Juba

K E N Y A

Kisumu *Mt. Kenya* ▲5,199 m

Lake Victoria

Tana

Nairobi

Kismayu

Mwanza

INDIAN OCEAN

▲ Kilimanjaro 5,895 m

Mombasa

SOMALIA

Mogadishu

SEYCHELLES

Dodoma

Zanzibar

BURUNDI

Dar-es-Salaam

TANZANIA

Rufiji

Aldabra Is.

SEYCHELLES

Lake Nyasa

MALAWI

C. Delgado

MALAWI

COMOROS

C. d'Ambre

Lilongwe

Moçambique

Antisiranana

Blantyre

MADAGASCAR

MOZAMBIQUE

Mahajanga

Toamasina

Beira

MAURITIUS

Antananarivo

MOZAMBIQUE

MADAGASCAR

MAURITIUS

Fianarantsoa

Réunion (France)

ZIMBABWE

C. Ste. Marie

Sting in the tail
Scorpions always look threatening. The curled-forward tail contains a sting which can be deadly. They eat insects and other animals which they catch with their claws. They are most common in desert areas.

FACT BOX

◆ **Central African Republic**
Area: 624,975 sq km
Population: 3,300,000
Capital: Bangui
Main language: French
Currency: Franc CFA

◆ **Gabon**
Area: 267,665 sq km
Population: 1,200,000
Capital: Libreville
Main language: French
Currency: Franc CFA

◆ **Republic of Congo**
Area: 342,000 sq km
Population: 2,500,000
Capital: Brazzaville
Main language: French
Currency: Franc CFA

◆ **Democratic Republic of Congo (Zaïre)**
Area: 2,345,410 sq km
Population: 46,500,000
Capital: Kinshasa
Main language: French
Currency: Zaïre

◆ **Rwanda**
Area: 26,330 sq km
Population: 6,900,000
Capital: Kigali
Main languages: Kinyarwanda, French
Currency: Rwanda franc

◆ **Burundi**
Area: 27,835 sq km
Population: 5,900,000
Capital: Bujumbura
Main languages: Kirundi, French
Currency: Burundi franc

◆ **Uganda**
Area: 236,580 sq km
Population: 22,000,000
Capital: Kampala
Main language: English
Currency: Uganda shilling

◆ **Kenya**
Area: 582,645 sq km
Population: 28,200,000
Capital: Nairobi
Main languages: Swahili, English
Currency: Kenya shilling

◆ **Somalia**
Area: 630,000 sq km
Population: 9,500,000
Capital: Mogadishu
Main languages: Somali, Arabic
Currency: Somali shilling

◆ **Tanzania**
Area: 939,760 sq km
Population: 29,100,000
Capital: Dodoma
Main languages: Swahili, English
Currency: Tanzanian shilling

◆ **Seychelles**
Area: 404 sq km
Population: 100,000
Capital: Victoria
Official languages: English, French, Creole
Currency: Seychelles rupee

◆ **Comoros**
Area: 1,860 sq km
Population: 600,000
Capital: Moroni
Official languages: Arabic, French
Currency: Comorian franc

◆ **Mauritius**
Area: 1,865 sq km
Population: 1,100,000
Capital: Port Louis
Official language: English

◆ **Madagascar**
Area: 594,180 sq km
Population: 15,200,000
Capital: Antananarivo
Official languages: Malagasy, French
Currency: Malagasy franc

◆ **Mozambique**
Area: 784,755sq km
Population: 16,500,000
Capital: Maputo
Official language: Portuguese
Currency: Metical

◆ **Malawi**
Area: 94,080 sq km
Population: 9,500,000
Capital: Lilongwe
Official language: Chichewa, English
Currency: Kwacha

◆ **Zambia**
Area: 752,615 sq km
Population: 9,200,000
Capital: Lusaka
Official language: English
Currency: Kwacha

◆ **Zimbabwe**
Area: 390,310 sq km
Population: 11,500,000
Capital: Harare
Official language: English
Currency: Zimbabwe dollar

◆ **Botswana**
Area: 575,000 sq km
Population: 1,500,000
Capital: Gaborone
Official language: English
Currency: Pula

◆ **Lesotho**
Area: 30,345 sq km
Population: 2,100,000
Capital: Maseru
Official languages: Sesotho, English
Currency: Loti

◆ **Swaziland**
Area: 17,365 sq km
Population: 1,000,000
Capital: Mbabane
Official languages: Swazi, English
Currency: Lilangeni

◆ **South Africa**
Area: 1,220,845 sq km
Population: 44,500,000
Capitals: Pretoria, Cape Town
Official languages: Afrikaans, English, Ndebele, Sesotho, Swazi, Tsonga, Tswana, Venda, Xhodsa, Zulu
Currency: Rand

◆ **Namibia**
Area: 824,295 sq km
Population: 1,600,000
Capital: Windhoek
Official language: English
Currency: Namibian dollar

◆ **Angola**
Area: 1,246,700 sq km
Population: 11,500,000
Capital: Luanda
Official language: Portuguese
Currency: Kwanza

AUSTRALIA

THIS COUNTRY is the size of a continent, a huge mass of land surrounded by ocean. The heart of **Australia** is a vast expanse of baking desert, salt pans, shimmering plains and dry scrubland. Ancient, rounded rocks glow in the morning and evening sun.

These barren lands are fringed by grasslands, tropical forests, creeks and fertile farmland. In the far east is the Great Dividing Range, which rises to the high peaks of the Australian Alps. The southeast is crossed by the Murray and Darling rivers. The Great Barrier Reef, the world's largest coral reef, stretches for over 2,000 kilometres off the eastern coast, while the island of Tasmania lies to the south across the Bass Strait.

Most Australians don't live in the 'outback', the dusty back country with its huge sheep and cattle stations and its mines. They live in big coastal cities such as Brisbane, Sydney, Adelaide and Perth. There they enjoy a high standard of living, an outdoor lifestyle, sunshine and surfing.

To the many people who in recent years have come from Europe and Asia to settle in Australia, this seems like a new country. However it is really a very ancient land, cut off from other parts of the world so long that it has many animals seen nowhere else on Earth, such as kangaroos, echidnas and platypuses.

Australia has probably been home to Aboriginal peoples for over 50,000 years. European settlement began in 1788, when the British founded a prison colony at Botany Bay, near today's city of Sydney. Many Australians still like to keep in touch with British relatives and traditions, but the modern country follows its own path as one of the great economic powers of the Pacific region.

Opera on the harbour

Sydney's most famous landmark is its Opera House, built between 1959 and 1973. It rises from the blue waters of the harbour like a great sailing ship. Sydney, the capital of New South Wales, is Australia's biggest city with a population of about 3,700,000.

Christmas beetles

Australia and its surrounding islands are populated by many weird and wonderful insects and beetles. These beetles are from Christmas Island.

Aboriginal art

An Aboriginal artist from Groote Eylandt, an island in the Gulf of Carpentaria, completes a painting on bark. Paintings by Australia's Aborigines are admired around the world. They often recall the ancient myths and legends of their people, with bold, swirling patterns or pictures of animals.

Bonaparte Archipelago

Broome

Fitzroy

Eighty Mile Beach

Port Hedland

De Grey

Barrow I.

Fortescue

Ashburton

Mt. Bruce

GIBSON DESERT

Lake Macleod

Carnarvon

Murchison

WESTERN AUSTRALIA

Dirk Hartog I.

Laverton

Geraldton

Kalgoorlie-Boulder

Perth

Fremantle

Bunbury

C. Naturaliste

Albany

C. Leeuwin

Archipelago of the Recherche

Torres Strait

Melville I.

Bathurst I.

Darwin

C. Arnhem

C. York

Joseph
Bonaparte
Gulf

Daly

Arnhem Land

Gulf of
Carpentaria

CAPE
YORK
PENINSULA

Drysdale

Roper

Groote
Eylandt

AUSTRALIA

Great Barrier Reef

KIMBERLEY
PLATEAU

Victoria

Wellesley Is.

Mitchell

Cairns

GREAT

BARKLY TABLELAND

Gilbert

NORTHERN
TERRITORY

Mount Isa

Flinders

Norman

Townsville

Proserpine

Mackay

GREAT
SANDY
DESERT

Georgina

QUEENSLAND

DIVIDING

C. Townsend

Rockhampton

MACDONNELL RANGES

Diamantina

Thomson

Belyando

RANGE

Bundaberg

Alice Springs

Barcoo

Uluru (Ayers Rock)
867m

SIMPSON
DESERT

Finke

Warrego

Culgoa

Brisbane

MUSGRAVE RANGES

Alberga

Toowoomba

GREAT
VICTORIA
DESERT

L. Eyre

Cooper Creek

Barwon

Gold Coast

SOUTH AUSTRALIA

Grafton

NULLABOR PLAIN

L. Everard

L. Torrens

Broken Hill

NEW SOUTH WALES

Coffs
Harbour

Great Australian Bight

L. Gairdner

FLINDERS
RANGE

Darling

Lachlan

Maitland

Newcastle

FACT BOX

◆ **Australia**
Area: 7,682,300 sq km
Population: 18,500,000
Capital: Canberra
Official language: English
Currency: Australian dollar

Port Lincoln

Spencer Gulf

Mildura

Adelaide

Wagga Wagga

GREAT DIVIDING RANGE

Sydney

Wollongong

Murray

Canberra AUSTRALIAN
CAPITAL
TERRITORY

Kangaroo I.

N

VICTORIA

Bendigo

Ballarat

Mt. Kosciusko
2,228m

C. Howe

Mount
Gambier

Geelong

Melbourne

C. Otway

Wilson's Promontory

TASMAN
SEA

Bass Strait

Flinders I.

King I.

Cape Barren I.

Burnie

Davenport

Launceston

TASMANIA

Queenstown

Hobart

South East C.

Cuddly koalas
The bear-like koala is found only
in Australia. It is a shy animal
which feeds by night on the
tender shoots of the eucalyptus
trees where it makes its home.
After its young are born, they
stay in a pouch in their mother's
body for about six months.

The big round up
Sheep are herded into pens before
shearing at an Australian sheep station.
Western Australia and New South Wales
have vast areas of countryside given
over to sheep rearing and wool is a
major export.

NEW ZEALAND AND THE PACIFIC

NEW ZEALAND LIES in the Pacific Ocean, about 1,600 kilometres to the east of Australia. It has a moist, mild climate and many unusual plants, birds and animals may be found there.

Most of its people live on North Island and South Island. These beautiful islands, divided by the Cook Strait, are the largest of several which are included within the country. North Island has volcanoes, hot springs and gushing geysers. South Island is dominated by the peaks and glaciers of the Southern Alps. It also has deep sea inlets called fiords and rolling grassy plains. New Zealand, with its sheep, cattle and fruit farms, has one of the most important economies in the Pacific region.

Papua New Guinea is another island nation, bordering Indonesian territory on the island of New Guinea. It also includes several chains of smaller islands. Many of its mountain regions, blanketed in tropical forests, were only opened up to the outside world in the 20th century. The country is rich in mineral resources and its fertile soils produce coffee, tea and rubber.

Strung out eastwards across the lonely Pacific Ocean are many scattered island chains and reefs. Small coral islands surround peaceful blue lagoons ringed with palm trees. The islanders may make their living by fishing, growing coconuts, mining or tourism. Many of the island groups have banded together to form independent nation states.

Peoples of the Pacific are of varied descent. Some are the descendants of European settlers – for example the British in New Zealand, or the French on New Caledonia or Tahiti. Fiji has a large population of Indian descent. The original peoples of the Pacific fall into three main groups. Melanesians, such as the Solomon Islanders, live in the western Pacific, while Micronesians live in the Caroline and Marshall Islands. The Polynesian peoples, brilliant seafarers, colonized vast areas of the ocean, from New Zealand to the Hawaiian Islands. The Maoris, who make up nine percent of New Zealand's population, are a Polynesian people who have kept and valued many of their ancient traditions.

SEA OF JAPAN

MICRONESIA

Yellow Sea

East China Sea

SOLOMON ISLANDS

Northern Mariana Islands (USA)

Philippine Sea

SOUTH CHINA SEA

Guam (USA)

Federated States of Micronesia

Celebes Sea

Palau

Papua New Guinea

Irian Jaya (Indonesia)

Arafura Sea

Port Moresby

Solomon Islands

Coral Sea

AUSTRALIA

TASMAN SEA

New Guinea finery
Feathers and paint are worn by many young warriors at tribal gatherings and feasts in remote areas of Papua New Guinea. The country has a very rich culture with over 860 different languages.

Kiwi fruit
When farmers decided to grow this fruit in New Zealand, they decided to give it a local name to help sales. The kiwi is the national bird, and a nickname for a New Zealander.

BERING SEA

PAPUA NEW
GUINEA

PALAU

N O R T H
P A C I F I C
O C E A N

Midway Island
(USA)

Wake Island
(USA)

MARSHALL
ISLANDS

Hawaii (USA)

VANUATU

Marshall Island

KIRIBATI

Nauru

NAURU

Kiribati

Tuvalu

TUVALU

SAMOA

Vanuatu

Samoa   American
Samoa

Fiji

French
Polynesia

S O U T H
P A C I F I C
O C E A N

Galapagos
(Ecuador)

New Caledonia
(France)

Cook Islands
(New Zealand)

Pitcairn Island
(UK)

Tonga

FIJI

TONGA

Easter Island
(Chile)

NEW ZEALAND

**NEW
ZEALAND**

FACT BOX

◆ **Papua New Guinea**
Area: 462,840 sq km
Population: 4,400,000
Capital: Port Moresby
Official language: English
Currency: Kina

◆ **New Zealand**
Area: 265,150 sq km
Population: 3,600,000
Capital: Auckland
Official language: English
Currency: New Zealand dollar

◆ **Palau**
Area: 490 sq km
Population: 16,000
Capital: Koror
Official languages: Palauan,
English
Currency: US dollar

◆ **Marshall Islands**
Area: 181 sq km
Population: 52,000
Capital: Majuro
Official language: Marshallese,
English
Currency: US dollar

◆ **Solomon Islands**
Area: 29,790 sq km
Population: 354,000
Capital: Honiara
Official language: English
Currency: Solomon Islands
dollar

◆ **Tuvalu**
Area: 25 sq km
Population: 13,000
Capital: Funafuti
Official languages: Tuvaluan,
English
Currency: Australian dollar

◆ **Kiribati**
Area: 684 sq km
Population: 75,000
Capital: Bairiki
Official language: English
Currency: Australian dollar

◆ **Nauru**
Area: 21 sq km
Population: 10,000
Capital: Yaren
Official language: Nauruan
Currency: Australian dollar

◆ **Fiji**
Area: 18,330 sq km
Population: 758,000
Capital: Suva
Official language: English
Currency: Fiji dollar

◆ **Tonga**
Area: 699 sq km
Population: 103,000
Capital: Nukualofa
Official languages: Tongan,
English
Currency: Pa'anga

◆ **Vanuatu**
Area: 14,765 sq km
Population: 156,000
Capital: Porta-Vila
Official languages: Bislama,
English, French
Currency: Vatu

◆ **Western Samoa**
Area: 2,840 sq km
Population: 170,000
Capital: Apia
Official languages: Samoan,
English
Currency: Tala

◆ **Federated States of
Micronesia**
Area: 702 sq km
Population: 114,000
Capital: Kolonia
Official language: English
Currency: US dollar

Easter Island
Hundreds of huge, mysterious stone heads tower above the hills of Easter Island, in the eastern Pacific. They were erected by Polynesians about 1,000 years ago. Today Easter Island is governed by Chile.

Gusher!
Steam bursts from volcanic rocks near Rotorua on North Island. New Zealand's geysers and hot springs are not just a tourist attraction. They are used to generate electricity.

NEW ZEALAND

North Cape

Whangerei

Gt. Barrier Island

Auckland
Manukau

Bay of
Plenty

East Cape

Hamilton

Rotorua

Gisborne

NORTH
ISLAND

Waikato

L. Taupo

New Plymouth

Ruapehu
2,797m

Napier

Wanganui

Hastings

Cape Farewell

Palmerston North

Nelson

Cook Strait

Wellington

Westport

Blenheim

Greymouth

SOUTH
ISLAND

SOUTHERN ALPS

Christchurch

Mt.Cook 3,764m

Canterbury
Plains

Timaru

Clutha

Dunedin

Foveaux Strait

Invercargill

Stewart Island

N

POLAR LANDS

THE NORTHERNMOST PART of our globe is called the Arctic. Within this bitterly cold region lie the northern borders of Alaska (part of the United States), Canada, Greenland (a self-governing territory of Denmark), Norway, Sweden, Finland and Russia.

However most of the area is covered by the Arctic Ocean, much of which is frozen solid all year round. At the centre of this great cap of ice is the North Pole. The **Arctic** supports a surprisingly wide selection of wildlife, including seals, walruses and polar bears. Peoples who have learned to live permanently in the far north include the Aleuts, the Inuit, the Saami, the Yakuts and the Chukchi. They have been joined in recent years by workers from the oil industry.

The only people to be found in **Antarctica**, at the other end of the globe, are scientists studying the weather and rocks of the coldest and windiest continent on Earth. The only other living things to survive here are the penguins which breed around the coast and the whales, birds and fishes of the Southern Ocean. The landmass is ringed by a shelf of ice, some of which breaks away to form massive icebergs in the spring. Inland there are mountain ranges and icy plains. The Antarctic winter takes place during the Arctic summer, and the Antarctic summer during the Arctic winter.

Various countries claim territory in Antarctica, and the continent is rich in minerals and fishing. However many scientists argue that this land should never be opened up to mining and industry, but left as the planet's last true wilderness.

Living in the Arctic
The Inuit peoples of northern Canada and Greenland have always lived by hunting and fishing and are experts at surviving in the harsh climate.

Antarctic melt
Each southern spring, the ice around Antarctica begins to melt, allowing ships to approach the ice shelves around this huge, frozen continent.

FACT BOX

◆ **Arctic Circle**
Area of ocean:
14,056,000 sq km

◆ **Antarctic Circle**
Area of land:
13,900,000 sq km

62

The publishers wish to thank the artists who have contributed to this book: Julie Banyard; Martin Camm; Mike Foster; Josephine Martin; Terry Riley; Guy Smith; Roger Smith; Michael White/Temple Rogers.

The publishers would like to thank the following for supplying photographs for the Atlas

Page 5 (T/R) MKP; 5 (B) PhotoDisc; 6-7, 9, 10-11 all MKP; 12 (C/R) & (B/L) Spectrum Colour Library; 14 (T/R) MKP; (B/L) & (B) The Stock Market; 15 (B) MKP; 17 (C/R) & B/R) The Stock Market; (B) MKP; 18 (B) MKP; (T/R) & (B/R) The Stock Market; 20-21, 24-25 all MKP; 26 (T/C) MKP; (B/C) The Stock Market; 28 (B/C) The Stock Market; 29 (T/R) The Stock Market; 30 both MKP; 32-33 (C) MKP; 33 (C) The Stock Market; 33 (B/R); MKP; 34 (T/L) MKP; 34 (B) The Stock Market; 35 (C) MKP; 37 (T/L) The Stock Market; (B/C) PhotoDisc; 38 (B/L) MKP; 39 (T/R) PhotoDisc; (C) & (B/R) The Stock Market; 40-41 all Sue Cunningham Photographic; 42-43 all MKP; 44 (T/L) MKP; 45 (C/R) The Stock Market; (B) MKP; 46 (T/R) The Stock Market; (B) & (B/C) MKP; 47 (C/R) MKP; 48 (T/R) & (C) MKP; 49 (C/R) MKP; (B/C) The Stock Market; 50-51 all MKP; 52-53 all MKP; 54-55 all The Stock Market; 56 (T/R) & (B/L) MKP; (B/C) The Stock Market; 58-59, 60-61 all MKP